THE
WEALTH
OF A
NATION

IN THE NATIONAL MUSEUMS
OF SCOTLAND

THE
WEALTH
OF A
NATION

IN THE NATIONAL MUSEUMS
OF SCOTLAND

edited by Jenni Calder

NATIONAL MUSEUMS OF SCOTLAND
EDINBURGH

RICHARD DREW PUBLISHING
GLASGOW

The exhibition 'The Wealth of a Nation' was held in the Royal Museum of Scotland, Chambers Street, Edinburgh, from 9 June to the 31 December 1989, with the generous sponsorship of the Royal Bank of Scotland.

Published by the National Museums of Scotland,
Chambers Street, Edinburgh EH1 1JF
and
Richard Drew Publishing Ltd,
6 Clairmont Gardens, Glasgow G3 7LW, Scotland.

© Copyright Trustees of the National Museums of Scotland 1989

British Library Cataloguing in Publication Data
The wealth of a nation.
   1. Scotland. Museums. National museums of Scotland. Stock
   I.   National Museums of Scotland 069'.09411

ISBN 0-86267-265-1 (Paperback)
ISBN 0-86267-267-8 (Hardback)

Designed by the Publications Office of the National Museums of Scotland
Typeset in Monophoto Lasercomp Garamond by
Advanced Filmsetters (Glasgow) Ltd
Printed and bound in Great Britain by Butler & Tanner Ltd, Frome and London

Front cover: gold lunula (collar) from Auchentaggart, Dumfriesshire, 2000 BC. The rich creativity of the Scottish people goes back at least 5000 years.

Frontispiece: Detail of the case of the silver travelling canteen of Prince Charles Edward Stuart, 1740–41.

Title page: Pictish silver armlet from the hoard found at Gaulcross, Banffshire, 7th–8th century AD.

CONTENTS

Acknowledgements

We would like to thank the many people who contributed text and information for this book, and helped in assembling the illustrations.

Except where otherwise acknowledged all the photographs were taken by Ian Larner, Ken Smith, Doreen Moyes, Joyce Smith and Lesley Boyle of the National Museums of Scotland photographic studio. Pictures credited 'SEA' are from the Museums' Scottish Ethnological Archive.

FOREWORD

To assess the true wealth of a nation, one does not call in an accountant; rather, one should consult the archaeologist and the antiquarian, the Finder and the Keeper. For the real resources of a nation are its people; and the story of that people is uttered through what they have left of themselves to posterity, the material of their culture, to be unearthed by the archaeologist, and cherished by the antiquarian, and illuminated by the scholar.

It is not artefacts that make a nation; but it is the artefacts made by people and for people that speak most clearly of the quality of that people, be they artists or engineers, peasants or poets, artisans or aristocrats, and provide tangible expressions of the qualities that have made Scotland the nation she is.

The National Museums of Scotland, of which I am a Trustee, have the finest and most extensive collections of Scottish material in existence. These collections form a marvellous treasury of Scotland's past, to be held in trust for the future. The function of a great national museum is to preserve and elucidate and present to the world that heritage of the hand, that patrimony of the intellect; for these collections form the landscapes of the past that it is the business of the museum to map.

It's a story that starts millions of years ago with the creation of Scotland as a landmass, with the rocks and minerals and fossils associated with its geological birth-pangs; it is these that explain Scotland's spectacular scenery and the life-forms that struggled for survival here. It's a story that charts the earliest beginnings of human activity in Scotland in the wake of the last Ice Age, of the peopling of Scotland nearly ten thousand years ago. It's a story that takes us through the dawn of what we are pleased to call civilization, from prehistoric farmers to Roman invaders, through

Picts and Celts and Norsemen to Scots and English, through the power-broking of princes and prelates, through early science and industrial innovation right up to our present technological world. It illustrates the lives and concerns and activities of the people of Scotland down the ages, the ordinary and the extraordinary, the famous and the infamous, the high and the humble.

But Scotland's past is not to be defined only within its own boundaries. A national museum also reflects a nation's place in the history of the wider world, the impact on civilization as a whole of Scotland's entrepreneurs and explorers, her scientists, her frontiersmen of the spirit, her 'worthies' in every sense of the term. They were purveyors of qualities and ideas and attitudes and products that had germinated in Scottish soil. The collections they acquired in foreign lands in which they pioneered new lives and livelihoods for themselves and for others – in North America and India, in Australia and Africa, in the Near and Far East – are just as illuminating about the intrinsic wealth of the nation as those from within Scotland's own borders.

Today museums are no longer dusty, echoing mausoleums full of ugly glass cases – what Sir Flinders Petrie once called 'ghastly charnel houses of murdered evidence'. Today the aim of the best museums is not only to care for their collections properly but also to promote public understanding and enjoyment by presenting them in, literally, their best light.

I have to admit that I do not believe that the National Museums of Scotland are equipped to do that properly – yet. This is by no means a criticism of the works of past Finders or present Keepers. In order to house and conserve and display the Wealth of the Nation as it deserves, we need a new Museum of Scotland building to give it the setting it deserves.

At no time in our history have we had an adequate home in which to display our wonderfully rich cultural heritage to its best advantage, and to the best advantage of the nation. At no time have we had a great national building in which to tell the story of Scotland's peoples and show all of her most treasured possessions. At present, only a small proportion of the National Museums' unrivalled Scottish collections can be seen by the public at any one time.

We have the treasures. In the National Museums we like to think we have the dedication, the motivation, and the necessary skills. We have the available site. All that is needed now is the concerted act of will to raise the funds needed to do the job.

The year 1991 will be the centenary of an important landmark in the story of the National Museums of Scotland. In 1891 the original National Museum of Antiquities of Scotland moved from the old Royal Institution at the foot of the Mound (now called the Royal Scottish Academy) to a handsome but impractical new building in Queen Street, through the huge generosity of John Ritchie Findlay, the proprietor of *The Scotsman* newspaper.

They don't make press barons like that any more. But they still make Scotsmen like that. Nothing would be a more fitting tribute to our past than to give it the future it deserves, in the kind of setting it deserves. Only a new and visionary Museum of Scotland will do full justice to the Scottish collections that make up the true Wealth of a Nation.

Magnus Magnusson

MUSEUMS IN THE MAKING

The origins and development of the national collections

RGW Anderson

Scotland's national collections have been developed over the past two centuries. They are now wide-ranging and possess considerable depth. Subjects covered are as diverse as archaeology, ethnology, sculpture and applied arts, numismatics, social and military history, history of science and technology, agriculture, geology and zoology. The National Museums of Scotland have interests which are international in scope, but not surprisingly a very particular concern is the material culture and natural history of Scotland herself. No other institution can approach the wealth and depth of these Scottish collections.

The National Museums of Scotland were set up in 1985 by the National Heritage (Scotland) Act, and were created by the amalgamation of two long-established institutions, the National Museum of Antiquities of Scotland which was founded in 1780, and the Royal Scottish Museum (first called the Industrial Museum of Scotland) which originated in 1854. The collections which had been amassed by these two parent organizations reflect the ages in which they were formed and the culture of those who had responsibilities for their curation. The earliest material to be incorporated were those parts of the seventeenth- and eighteenth-century natural history collections which still survived in the University of Edinburgh in the middle of the nineteenth century, at which time they were handed over to government. These collections embodied the spirit of discovery of the natural world in the late Renaissance, when geographical exploration of the New World stimulated interest in the environment at home. The collections formed by the Society of Antiquaries of Scotland were in the catholic tradition of eighteenth-century antiquarianism, a wide range of objects being acquired for discussion, research and

'A Fat and Lean Antiquarian' from *The Antiquarian Repertory, compiled by Francis Grose, Thomas Astle, and others*, 1807.

The Main Hall of the Royal Museum of Scotland, Chambers Street, designed by Francis Fowke and built in the 1860s and '70s.

David Stewart Erskine, 11th Earl of
Buchan: portrait in oils by James Wales
after Sir Joshua Reynolds, about 1780.

preservation. The Industrial Museum of Scotland reflected the will
of government, following the Great Exhibition of 1851, to expand
education and to promote information about manufacturing
processes. All these collections were carefully developed and
husbanded until now they number more than three million
individual items, providing unique historical records, research
resources, educational possibilities and visual excitement.

It was partly to prevent the disposal and destruction of
collections that the Society of Antiquaries of Scotland was
established in the first place. Two important Scottish collections,
those of Sir Andrew Balfour (1630–94) and Sir Robert Sibbald
(1641–1722), had been bequeathed to the University of Edinburgh
but within the space of fifty years they had been dispersed. This
was a matter of concern to David Stewart Erskine, 11th Earl of
Buchan, and he called a meeting at his house at 21 St Andrew
Square, Edinburgh, on 14 November 1780 at which he declared,
'It has long been a subject of regret that no regular society for
promoting antiquarian researches has subsisted in this part of
Great Britain.' He was well aware of the activities of the Society
of Antiquaries of London which had been founded in 1707 and
which started to form its collection shortly afterwards, accumulating miscellaneous antiquities and works of art as adjuncts to
its library.

At the third meeting, on 18 December 1780, the new Society
of Antiquaries of Scotland was formally instituted and almost
immediately a museum was initiated. The first objects were
recorded by the Society in January 1781 and included fifty-three
late bronze age weapons (called at the time a 'Quantity of Roman
Arms') which had been dredged up from Duddingston Loch
near Edinburgh. Today fifty-one of these pieces still survive, a
remarkable fact which vindicates Buchan's hopes for permanence.
Early collecting was not, however, particularly biased towards
archaeology; it was projected on a broad basis in the spirit of
eighteenth-century antiquarianism and fascination with the natural
world. Material sought after by the Antiquaries, and frequently
donated to the embryo museum, included books, manuscripts,
objects of prehistoric, Roman, Viking and medieval origin, ethno-
graphical artefacts, and the basis of a natural history collection.
These acquisitions were by no means confined to objects with
Scottish connections. In 1784, for example, donations included a
book published in Venice, Russian coins, Danish seals, a Chinese
map and, of origin unknown, 'A crow dried, having three legs and

feet of equal size'. A number of ethnological items which were donated in July 1781, including a tool embedded with shark's teeth from Hawaii and reed pan-pipes from Tonga, came from Captain Cook's third voyage to the Pacific Ocean.

The Antiquaries' collection was shunted round a good deal in the early years, from one Edinburgh house to another, from Old Town to New Town. The constraints of space had an effect on activities, though some types of object were being collected in considerable numbers. In 1819 the curator, James Skene, reported that the collection of coins and medals 'consists of Scottish and English Coins, pretty complete, Roman, Greek, a mess of foreign coins of most of the European nations, and a few Oriental'. In 1826 the government provided the Society with rooms in the newly built Royal Institution (now called the Royal Scottish

Part of the hoard of late bronze age
weapons found in Duddingston Loch,
near Edinburgh in 1780.

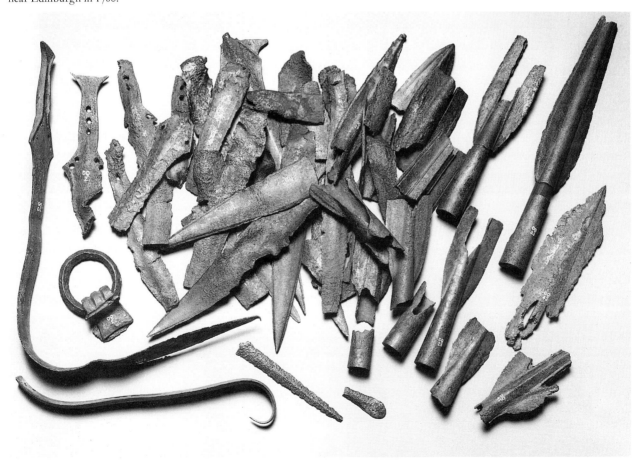

Academy) at the foot of the Mound in Princes Street. Acquisitions of new material revived. Skene reported, when the Museum was reopened, 'As a greater extent was obtained for the display of the various articles of the Museum, and much care was exercised in their exposure and arrangement, the Public soon perceived that their donations were duly appreciated, and valuable additions began rapidly to flow in.' At this time the very important twelfth-century bronze shrine containing an iron bell, from Kilmichael Glassary, Argyll, was acquired, and in 1831 the Hunterston brooch was placed on display.

After the first fifty years of accumulating a wide range of objects, there was change and refinement in collecting. The first part of the collection to be transferred was the natural history material, which was accepted by the Royal Society of Edinburgh in 1828. In the following century charters and documents were sent to the Scottish Record Office, books and manuscripts went to the National Library of Scotland, Egyptian, Greek and Roman antiquities, together with non-European ethnological material, were transferred to the Royal Scottish Museum, and drawings and paintings were deposited in the Scottish National Portrait Gallery.

In the 1830s and '40s the financial problems of maintaining the collection loomed large. Fellows rallied, debts were paid off, and in 1849 the first catalogue of the Museum was published. The revival was largely due to the work of Daniel Wilson, who used the Danish system of classification of archaeological artefacts in the stone, bronze and iron age periods – he was the first British archaeologist to do so. But it was clear that an unsubsidized society could not bear the burden of the Museum and negotiations were set in motion to transfer responsibility to the government. These arrangements were concluded in 1858 and the Museum was reopened to great public interest. A plea was made for additional material by Sir James Young Simpson who, though better known as the discoverer of chloroform as an anaesthetic, was also an important amateur archaeologist:

> In pleading with the Scottish public for the augmentation and enrichment of our Museum by donations of all kinds ... we plead for what is not any more the property of this Society, but what is now the property of the Nation.... Single specimens and examples of archaeological relics are in the hands of a private individual generally nought but mere matters of idle curiosity and wild conjecture; while all of them become of use, and sometimes of great moment, when placed in a public collection beside their fellows.

Collecting gathered pace during the second half of the nineteenth century. The Keeper of the Museum from 1869 to 1913, Joseph Anderson, was particularly acquisitive: by 1887, calculations showed that there were 25,104 implements and objects of stone, 1394 objects of bronze, 4137 domestic remains from hut-circles, brochs and lake dwellings, 7107 ecclesiastical and medieval items, and 7192 'miscellaneous'. Anderson himself was involved in archaeological fieldwork, an activity which was to increase the holdings of the Museum substantially. But items were being purchased, amongst them some of the most renowned pieces, for example the Hunterston brooch (£500 in 1831) and some of the Lewis chessmen (£105 in 1891). In spite of this activity it must be said that the Museum's collecting policy remained somewhat restricted.

In 1891 the Museum left the Mound for the new building in Queen Street provided through the munificence of John Ritchie Findlay, proprietor of *The Scotsman*, and shared with the Scottish National Portrait Gallery. The displays in Queen Street are clearly defined by the published catalogue issued in the following year. Apart from a small separate section on the second floor, 'Collections from other Countries for Comparison', the exhibition was purely of Scottish objects and of objects from Scottish locations. The contemporary museum philosophy developed by General A H Lane-Fox Pitt-Rivers, of showing objects of similar function from different cultural origins, was strictly not adopted in the Museum of Antiquities. No doubt it was affected by the existence of the Edinburgh Museum of Science and Art, open to the public from 1866, which had been collecting world-wide since its foundation.

There were, however, changes in acquisitions policy at Queen Street from the almost undeviating attention to archaeology and early antiquities. Increasingly, post-medieval objects were added to the collections. When acting as Director during the Second World War, the archaeologist V Gordon Childe accepted eighteenth-century costume. Towards the end of the 1950s collections of agricultural and rural crafts were developed and the acquisition pattern became much more balanced, allowing for exhibitions of greater chronological and cultural spread. The idea of a separate agricultural museum was mooted following successful temporary displays at the Royal Highland and Agricultural Society's Show at Ingliston, just outside Edinburgh, in the 1960s. Eventually, after supporters had established the

The National Museum of Antiquities at the Royal Institution on the Mound, with Joseph Anderson and George Black, 1890.

Hugh Miller's winged fish, *Pterich-thyodes*. A rare example from the Middle Old Red Sandstone (about 380 million years ago) of Lethen Bar, Nairnshire, showing two specimens each 100 mm long. **Fishes: fossil**

Gordon Childe at Skara Brae, Orkney, 1920s.

Scottish Country Life Museum Trust, a permanent building was provided which opened to the public in 1982.

This broader activity did not mean a diminution of traditional interests. In the 1920s Gordon Childe dug at the celebrated neolithic site at Skara Brae in Orkney (a site further developed by David Clarke in the 1970s) and the finds were deposited in the Museum of Antiquities. A O Curle, who had previously been Director at Queen Street before moving to Chambers Street, uncovered the buildings at Jarlshof in Shetland in the 1930s and again finds were deposited. However there were certainly areas of neglect for a museum which might aspire to provide an overview of Scottish culture, for example heavy engineering and transport.

These topics were left to the attention of the Royal Scottish Museum, so it is necessary at this point to consider where Scotland's other national museum fits into the collecting picture. Profits from the highly successful Great Exhibition of 1851 were

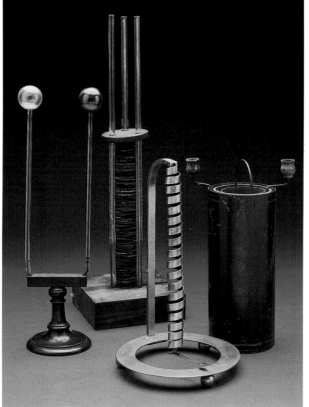

The brooch from Hunterston, Ayrshire, one of the great pieces of Hiberno-Saxon metalwork, about AD 700. **Pseudo-penannular brooches**

Army Gold Cross, 1811–14, with 6 clasps. **Military orders, decorations and medals**

Apparatus from the Playfair Collection: early 19th-century voltaic pile, Sturgeon cell, after 1824, 19th-century differential thermoscope and demonstration model of a bimetallic spiral thermometer, about 1830. **Chemical apparatus; History of physical science**

used to finance the newly-formed Department of Science and Art, which set up museums with strongly educational functions in London (the South Kensington Museum) and in Edinburgh. The Secretary of the Department, Lyon Playfair, was a graduate of Edinburgh University and while a student he had developed a strong friendship with a fellow medical student George Wilson (brother of Daniel), who later became a private teacher of chemistry. Wilson was appointed Director of the Industrial Museum in 1855, and his zealous attitude to its didactic function had a strong influence on the development of the early collections. The aim of the new Museum had been argued by Playfair in the following (rather geological) terms:

George Wilson, Director of the Industrial Museum of Scotland, 1855–59. (*National Galleries of Scotland*)

> The establishment of such an institution in the capital of Scotland would be of great national benefit by affording the means of obtaining definite information in regard to the mineral wealth of this kingdom, its ores and coals, its building, paving and ornamental stones, granites and marbles, the localities and composition of soils, the qualities and capabilities of its different clays for bricks, tiles or pottery wares, and of its limestones for building purposes and manure and generally as a means of developing the industrial resources of its territorial products.

Wilson certainly concerned himself with these matters but he took an interest in manufactures as well as the raw materials. He expressed his policy in a rather simple statement, 'The Industrial Museum is not intended to be a museum of Scottish industry alone, but a museum of the industry of the world in special relation to Scotland.'

Wilson remained in office for only four years; he died in 1859. Nevertheless he collected enthusiastically for his new Museum, which started from nothing. The Annual Report following his death gives statistics of acquisitions made up till then. They are categorized as follows:

I	Models, implements	350
II	Specimens of economic geology, including the Arts dealing with mineral products	6,000
III	Specimens of economic botany, including the Arts dealing with vegetable products	2,800
IV	Specimens of economic zoology, including the Arts dealing with animal products	1,200
	Total models and specimens	10,350

Among the items acquired by Wilson might be mentioned a large collection of 'Scottish Rock Specimens' from the Highland and Agricultural Society (representing raw materials) and 'A set of golf balls, illustrating an abandoned application of feathers which, before the introduction of gutta percha, were employed in stuffing them' (representing the industrial arts). But much was acquired which was not of Scottish origin: a collection of rocks from southern Africa donated by David Livingstone and 'Indian and Esquimaux models and specimens from the Hudson's Bay Territories'.

The use to which the collections were put sharply contrasted with the practice in the Museum of Antiquities, where objects were used in research and were frequently published in the Proceedings of the Society. Wilson spent much of his time teaching, using his objects as visual aids. The classes were attended, Wilson wrote, by those in the legal, military and medical professions; engineers, dyers, paper-makers, silk weavers, merchants, farmers and teachers; those who were preparing to emigrate to the colonies; and 'amateurs unconnected specially with any calling'. Wilson was aware, however, of the historical value of his material and he was particularly interested in the history of science and technology. In 1857 he wrote:

> An Industrial Museum cannot be complete without historical illustrations of the progress of the useful arts. Accordingly, the Director has solicited contributions of examples exhibiting the early forms of important instruments, and has begun by presenting an antique working model of the first glass friction electrical machine.

A year later he acquired from Lyon Playfair what is now appreciated as one of the finest collections of early chemical apparatus to survive.

The Industrial Museum was only part of the new enterprise in Scotland initiated by the government. In 1855 the natural history collections of Edinburgh University were transferred to ownership of the Department of Science and Art by the patrons of the University, the Town Council of Edinburgh, the intention being that when a building was constructed for the Museum, they would be displayed alongside the industrial collections. This was much against the wishes of the University.

The University natural history collections had their origins in the seventeenth-century collections of Sir Andrew Balfour and Sir

Robert Sibbald. Of these, Daniel Defoe in 1727 said that, 'It contains a vast treasure of curiosities of Art and Nature, domestic and foreign from almost all Parts of the World; and is greatly valued by the Virtuosoes containing some Rarities that are not to be found either in those of the Royal Society at London or the Ashmolean at Oxford'. The collection was not adequately cared for by the University and in 1779 the professor of natural history, the Reverend John Walker, discarded much on the grounds that 'The greater part of it is mere rubbish that can never be of any use'. Walker set about rebuilding the collection methodically but the cycle repeated itself on his death in 1803. Part was removed from the University by his trustees, and Walker's successor, Robert Jameson, ejected much of the remainder.

Yet another collection was built up, this one proving more permanent. In 1812 Jameson appealed to the Crown for money and he secured an annual grant of £100 to cover expenses in securing and preserving specimens. Several years later a major collection was added, that of the French naturalist Louis Dufresne, as well as a selection of William Bullock's exhibits from the Egyptian Hall in Piccadilly. The baby African elephant from Bullock's collection remains a favourite display item today.

At Jameson's insistence the collection was put on display to the public in 1820 in the new University building originally designed by Robert Adam and finished by William Playfair (now called 'The Old Quad'). Jameson had high ambitions, referring in 1826 to his enterprise as 'The National Museum of this Country'. He died in 1854, and the chair was held briefly by Edward Forbes until his premature death in the following year. The terms of the transfer of the collection to the government were that the professor of natural history would continue to be in charge of the collections, now numbering 74,000 specimens, geological and zoological, and would be known as Regius Keeper. The arrangement also specified that the collections would be freely available for teaching University students. The objects themselves were not moved with the change of ownership as there was nowhere for them to be moved to: the foundation of the Industrial Museum did not mean that purpose-built accommodation was provided immediately. In 1861 a building was started adjacent to the University and five years later the first phase of it was opened. A bridge was constructed to join the University to the new Museum to give students access to the natural history collections. The Industrial Museum of Scotland and the Natural History

'Black's glass' from the Playfair Collection of 18th-century chemical glassware.

The scientific staff of the Scottish National Antarctic Expedition on board SY *Scotia*. Material from this expedition came to the Museum. Photographed by W S Bruce.

Museum were brought together and were renamed the Edinburgh Museum of Science and Art.

The relationship between the director, who had responsibility for the industrial arts, and the professor of natural history, who had to use his collections for research and teaching students as well as for public display, soon became strained. This came to a head in the early 1870s, when the director, Thomas Archer, and the regius professor, Charles Wyville Thomson, engaged in a dispute over the arrangement of the natural history material and the disposal of duplicates in the former University collection. The row reached farcical levels: Archer changed the locks on the doors of the bridge after he claimed that students had stolen the refreshments provided for a band playing at a conversazione in the Museum. In 1873 a Commission reported to the Department of Science and Art that the administrative arrangements between the University and Museum should be changed and that a full-time Keeper of Natural History should be appointed who would report to the Director.

Collecting of zoological and botanical specimens, fossils and minerals was active throughout the nineteenth century and seems not to have suffered as a result of the problems and jealousies. In fact the basis for the current collection of nearly three million specimens was laid at the time. In spite of the problems, the Challenger expedition under the leadership of Wyville Thomson, conducted from 1872, eventually resulted in some collections of marine material being acquired by the Museum, some via the British Museum. This was followed by the Scottish National Antarctic Expedition of 1902–4, conducted by William Speirs Bruce in the sailing yacht *Scotia*, which led to the deposit of fish, invertebrates and mollusca in the Museum. The tradition continues today with the Museum involvement in Marine Biological Association expeditions to collect midwater fishes in the north-east Atlantic. Research collections have been added at regular intervals in recent years: Kenneth Morton's collection of world dragonflies (1940), Jeremy Anderson's reptiles from Pakistan (1962), the Rev William and Dr William Searle's birds' eggs (1987), and Robert Stebbings' collection of British and European bats (1988). These collections are frequently used by research scientists who publish papers based on the reference material (and who often donate their own collections to the Museum).

The story of the geological collections has not been dissimilar. The Scottish mineral collection was based on two major donations in the nineteenth century: Patrick Dudgeon's collection acquired in 1878 (at the time the second most extensive collection in existence) followed in 1894 by Professor Forster Heddle's (*the* most extensive); the latter was purchased for £1000, of which £640 was raised by public subscription. 'The result,' boasted the director in his annual report, 'will be one of the finest national collections in existence of the minerals of any single country.' With this collection coexisted the rocks and fossils, maps and diagrams of the Geological Survey, which were housed in the newly-completed West Wing from 1889. In 1906 all geological material was brought together to form a Geological Department for the first time. Even today, new species of minerals are still occasionally discovered by museum staff and there is sophisticated equipment at Chambers Street to analyse their structure. The fossil collection also has internationally recognized strengths, especially the Old Red Sandstone and Carboniferous fossil fishes. The famous collection formed by Hugh Miller was purchased by public subscription in 1859 and many further specimens were subsequently added: scarcely a year went by without an important group of specimens being added. The Museum continues to conduct its own fieldwork, and current finds of fossils of early

Hugh Miller, whose collection of fossils, of major scientific importance, was acquired in 1859. (*National Galleries of Scotland*)

amphibia from East Kirkton, near Bathgate, are proving to be of crucial significance.

In the early twentieth century there was a gradual redefinition of the word 'art' as it applied to museum collections. The change of policy was largely due to new attitudes adopted by Robert Murdoch Smith, director from 1885. 'Industrial art' tended to be downgraded and frequently de-accessioned, while decorative art took its place. Even the large collection of 600 items from the Wedgwood factory ('wares illustrating the ceramic art ... raw materials, vessels in their different styles, moulds, models of furnaces') acquired in 1856 was largely thrown out in 1940. Donations from the great exhibitions in the latter part of the nineteenth century would be very lucky to survive disposal boards of the 1920s and 1950s. On the other hand, collections of non-European ethnology and oriental art were added, the Museum benefiting from the traditional travels of Scots to the far corners of the earth. Murdoch Smith himself brought back collections of Persian art. In recent years it has occasionally been possible to send curators to, for example, the Near East to collect rugs, and to the South Pacific to collect canoes.

More traditional 'art museum' collecting has been conducted throughout the twentieth century. In 1905 the collection of arms and armour formed by Sir J Noel Paton was sold to the Museum for the (then huge) sum of £10,000. During the Second World War a magnificent bequest of gold snuff boxes was made by J Cathcart White. By and large the Royal Scottish Museum tended to collect non-Scottish art objects but there were exceptions: the Watson mazer of about 1515, the first Scottish mazer in a public collection, was purchased in 1948; and there were other major acquisitions of items archetypically Scottish such as communion tokens and bagpipes. In recent years areas of excellence have become focused: for example, French silver. Napoleon's tea service and Princess Pauline Borghese's travelling *nécessaire* have been purchased. These are obviously not of Scottish origin but they have very strong Scottish connections through the 10th Duke of Hamilton (admirer of the Emperor and close friend of the Princess) and have resided in Scotland since 1830.

The technology collection of the Royal Scottish Museum was intended to be of international origin but in practice was largely of British, if not of Scottish, manufacture. As in many science museums in the twentieth century, there was an emphasis on stationary engines and the 'Machinery Hall' became known as

Early photograph of the locomotive
Wylam Dilly while still in use at Wylam
Colliery, Northumberland.

'The Hall of Power'. Again, as with other similar museums, model-making became an important activity and the Industrial Museum workshop opened as early as 1866. Model ships were added in large numbers and became an art-form in themselves. There was relatively little effort to collect transport items, though 'Wylam Dilly', a William Hedley locomotive of 1813 (along with 'Puffing Billy' the oldest to survive in the world) was a major acquisition in 1882. Perhaps the greatest strength of the technological collections has always been the lighthouse collection, deposited over the years by the Commissioners of the Northern Lighthouses from 1875.

Collections of scientific instruments started at a relatively late stage. Concerted efforts were not made until the 1960s, though the current collection has been built up to be one of the best in the United Kingdom. Perhaps quite naturally it has an unmatched collection of Scottish-made instruments, the earliest known example being a circular slide rule and sundial constructed for the latitude of Edinburgh by Robert Davenport in about 1650. The splendid collection of demonstration apparatus from the Natural Philosophy Department of Edinburgh University, acquired in 1972, is an indication of the importance and quality of science teaching in Scottish universities from the early eighteenth century. Strong efforts have been made to collect recent scientific apparatus: the Cockcroft-Walton accelerator from Edinburgh and part of the Glasgow Synchrotron started the policy of collecting in this vitally significant, if unfashionable, field. A fine collection of computers has been established. Surely this is an undeniably important class of artefact: but can they ever be considered to be visually stimulating enough for display?

In addition to the longer-established collections in Queen Street and Chambers Street (to which now are added outstations: the Scottish Agricultural Museum at Ingliston, the Museum of Flight at East Fortune, Biggar Gas Works, and Shambellie House Museum of Costume at New Abbey) a further, major museum has been built up in Edinburgh since 1930 and now is part of the National Museums of Scotland. This is the Scottish United Services Museum, originally the Scottish Naval and Military Museum and seen as part of the act of commemoration for Scottish servicemen killed in the Great War. On its foundation, many

Medals and *in memoriam* card of Private Alexander Keay, Royal Army Medical Corps, killed in action at the Ypres Salient, 5 October 1917.

Three-compartment parcel-gilt table snuff box made by A G Wighton, Edinburgh, associated with the Edinburgh squadron of the Royal Midlothian Yeomanry, 1837.

significant historical items were donated and the Museum built an extremely fine collection of Scottish military uniform, for which it is widely known. Other areas of collecting were pursued: edged weapons and firearms, medals, paintings and prints of military concern. On the change of name in 1948, Royal Air Force interests were incorporated.

In 1970 the Royal Scottish Museum incorporated the Scottish United Services Museum, the military collections benefiting from access to a larger purchase grant. In recent years this has been used to build up the strength of the medal collection, of military musical instruments, and of 'Services art' such as presentation silver. Unexpected finds are still possible: a unique seventeenth-century Scots officer's mitre cap, sold as a tea cosy, was acquired in 1985. Collecting post-1918 objects connected with warfare poses particular problems, especially of size and conservation. The Museum has yet to acquire a tank or a battleship – and it is unlikely to do so. Military aircraft have been collected. There are a Spitfire and a Vulcan bomber to be seen at East Fortune, alongside civilian aircraft, aero engines and rockets.

The Antiquaries who collected the Duddingston Loch bronze age weapon hoard in 1780 and the curators who acquired the Vulcan bomber in 1984 did not unthinkingly preserve that which happened to be available. They were imbued with the cultural values of their time, and their collections reflect different views of the past. Thus the objects indicate the contemporary attitudes of their collectors and add a further dimension which, if interpreted, can provide historical evidence beyond that which is encapsulated in the material culture or scientific object itself. We are fortunate indeed that we possess this long, continuous, rich inheritance spreading over two centuries. It can be seen to represent the intellectual, natural and economic Wealth of a Nation.

ESSENTIAL EVIDENCE
The material culture of Scotland

Alexander Fenton

The Scottish collections in the National Museums of Scotland cover over six thousand years of time. In spite of gaps – for who can collect everything? – they are amongst the most representative of any national collection anywhere. They mark the life and work and artistic aspirations of our predecessors, their craftmanship and their ability to use what the environment provided. They chart the movements of peoples into Scotland, and the differences in social status, and they contain the paraphernalia of administration, religion and education. In short, they encapsulate all the complex interlocking factors that go into the making of a nation. Like a three-dimensional lexicon, museum collections are a key to a country's history. But objects, like words, have to be interpreted. They have to be put into their contexts in time, space and social setting before their full meaning can be extracted.

The basic stock of material culture collections in national museums is divided, in the conventional view, into two broad phases: prehistoric and historical, that is, before and after the appearance of written records. The historical period is reckoned as coming with the Romans. However, written records were few then and remained so for centuries. Archaeology has most to tell us of the Romans and their precursors in Scotland. It is relatively less informative on the centuries following their departure. In considering phases of material culture, we find a pattern that is more complicated than the simple division between prehistory and history. It is more meaningful to divide periods into six overlapping and interlocking phases: prehistory including the Roman period, the post-Roman period to the twelfth century, the Middle Ages, the early modern period to the beginnings of industrialization, the period of industry and empire, and finally, the present day.

Stone circle at Callanish, Isle of Lewis.
(SDD: Historic Buildings and Monuments Division)

Spinning with distaff and spindle at
Black Corries, Glencoe, Argyll, 1897.
*(Original photograph by Lady Henrietta
Gilmour; Sir Ian Gilmour, Bart, Montrave;
SEA)*

Prehistory

Because of the lack of written records, prehistoric material must be interpreted in ways different from those possible with the aid of documentation. One approach is to look at still-functioning survivals in this and other countries. If we do this, the projection back in time of practices relating to present-day or recent tools and equipment of traditional character must always be done with great care. This is true whether we are looking at food-processing techniques in the remoter parts of the land, such as means of drying cereal grains without using a built stone kiln, or at technological practices such as the flaking of flint and quartz to make arrowheads and scrapers, the hafting of axes, the shaping and firing of pottery, the processing of ores and metals to make weapons, tools and other items, and the spinning and weaving of textiles.

From Victorian times it became fashionable to seek out comparisons, whether amongst survivals of the past into the present in our own country or amongst the distant nations of the world, on the basis of the intellectual concept of man's rise from savagery to civilization. The fashion died, though archaeologists may still turn to ethnographic evidence for information about techniques and functions that will allow them at least to narrow the range of options in their efforts to interpret the past.

In fact, prehistorians have to work very hard to interpret their material. Besides examination of recent survivals, they use or have used devices that range from comparative typology to modern scientific means of study like thermoluminescence, radiocarbon dating, dendrochronology, X-ray fluorescence, neutron activation and the like. They use the knowledge of geologists in seeking, for example, the sources of deposits from which steatite pots, clay vessels, stone axes and quern-stones were made, of botanists in identifying the impressions of cereal grains and weed seeds left on the outsides of fired pots, and in analyzing the micro-flora and pollen remains in excavations, and of natural historians for microfauna.

Such work in partnership is greatly enhancing the depth of the archaeological record. It is also teaching us how to read more clearly the changing landscape of human settlement from its beginnings, and to assess the effects of man on his early environment. It helps us to produce at least relative chronologies for the tools, equipment, containers and other items associated

The Hunterston brooch: detail from the back of this 8th-century brooch showing the later runic inscription.

with ever intensifying phases of settlement. Sociologists and social anthropologists too, with their concern for communities and social interaction, for symbols of power and status, for acculturation and diffusion and internal colonialism, can also help at least to give reasoned parameters to speculation about the human systems of the almost unknowable past.

What is emerging is a curious sense of sophistication, given the limits of available knowledge and materials, even in early times. A light, symmetrical cultivating implement, the ard, seems to go as far back as the beginnings of cultivation; there is no clear evidence for a long preceding period when men grew tired of prodding the soil with digging sticks. The building of Stonehenge, or of the standing stones of Callanish, needed much more than brute strength. The Victorian concept of the long, slow advance from savagery is dead. We have gained respect for those we are now pleased to call our ancestors.

The Roman period to the twelfth century

Historians, especially those of the medieval period, are increasingly learning to apply techniques of investigation that were often first developed for prehistoric interpretation. Such cross-fertilization can only be for good, in our efforts to understand the material culture of past times. In any case, we still have to depend heavily on archaeology for the early medieval period.

There was indeed writing of more than one kind. Latin inscriptions were left by the Romans who occupied parts of Scotland between AD 80 and about AD 200 and campaigned sporadically until about AD 390. Latin was also used in inscriptions of the church from about AD 400. There was Irish ogam lettering consisting of coded series of strokes on carved stones of the seventh and eighth centuries and on smaller objects, for example a bone knife handle from North Uist in the Hebrides. There was Scandinavian runic writing on carved stones, as on the walls of the Maeshowe tomb in Orkney that was broken into by Vikings in the twelfth century, and also as found scratched as a tenth-century addition to the back of the Hunterston brooch (about AD 700). But such records are normally terse, if we can understand them at all, and indicate little more than ownership or commemoration. We can be sure that the ability to produce and read these was chiefly a function of a learned class.

Pictish stone carved with a goose and a fish (probably a salmon), from Easterton of Roseisle, Morayshire, 7th–8th century AD.

But it is on such sources, and on sculptured stones and metalwork, that we have to depend for knowledge of cultural levels of at least the higher echelons of society in the centuries between the collapse of the Roman Empire and the full Middle Ages. For this period – and this is a phenomenon common to other countries – the evidence of archaeology is of little help. It has been a major task for scholars to take the 'dark' out of the 'Dark Ages'. Though archaeology is producing increasing amounts of data, it is the surviving material culture that continues to speak to us with the loudest voice.

The mask of the Rev Alexander
Peden, Covenanting minister, late 17th
century. **Memorabilia**

In fact, Scotland can be exempted from the description 'Dark Ages' applied to Europe in the wake of the Roman Empire. Scotland was not overrun by barbarian hordes and, in contrast, made unique contributions to the cultural history of Europe in the period. It is clear that basic skills were not lost. Along with writing of three kinds, the spread of Christianity from Celtic church foundation to re-evangelize much of Europe and the first shaping of an organized kingdom, there was a flourishing artistic culture that could produce outstanding objects, such as the great silver chains decorated with Pictish motifs picked out in red enamel, and the corpus, exceptional in Europe, of Pictish sculptured stones with their still mysterious symbolism. The brooches from Hunterston (about AD 700) and Rogart (about AD 800) are outstanding by any standard. The St Ninian's Isle treasure, buried about AD 800 in Shetland against the arrival of the Norse, tells much about the metalwork of the period and about the movements of pieces, and with them artistic ideas, from other countries. The Monymusk reliquary of about AD 750, the Brecbennoch of St Columba, which the Abbot of Abroath brought as a revered relic to the battle of Bannockburn in 1314, is among the most precious historical and Christian treasures in our collections. With it go the eleventh-century crosier of St Fillan called the *Coicrich*, of Scottish or Irish origin, and St Fillan's twelfth-century bell, as outstanding relics of the Celtic church.

Silver-gilt sword chapes, which
strengthened the scabbard, from the
Pictish treasure found on St Ninian's
Isle, Shetland.

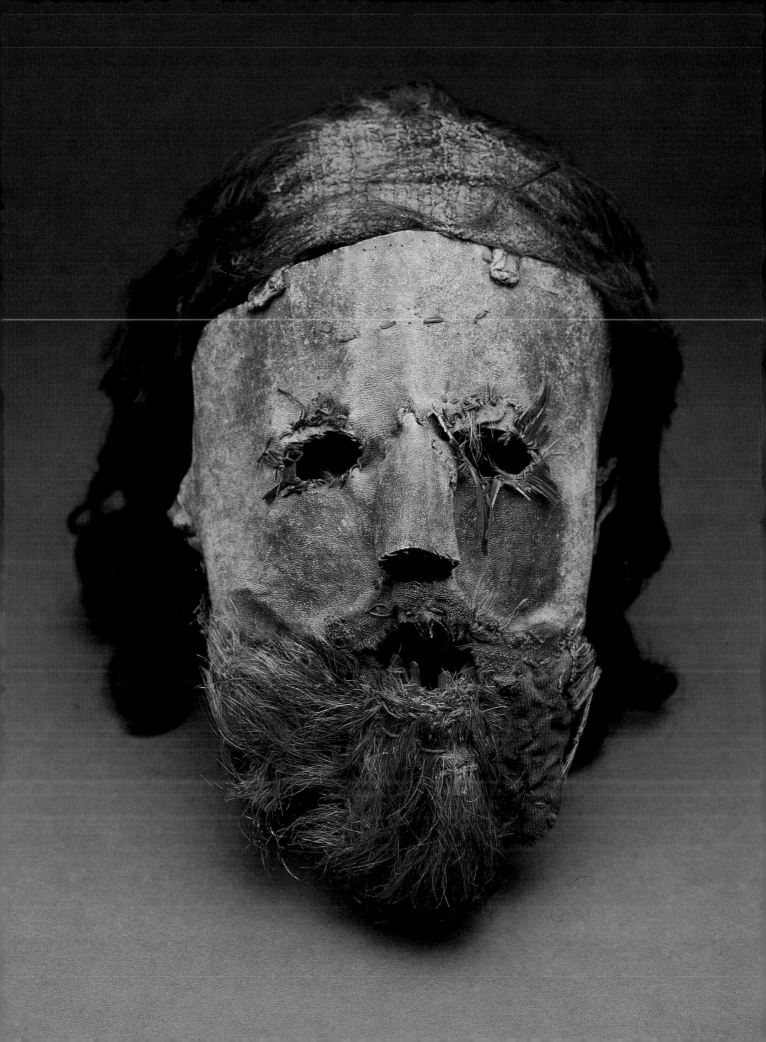

The Monymusk reliquary: a portable
house shrine, about AD 750, known as
the Brecbennoch of St Columba. **Early
Christianity; Pre-Reformation church
furnishings and relics**

Watercolour of pair of Clydesdales in
show harness, painted in Banffshire, 1910,
by the horseman who looked after them.
Man and beast

Far right Viking jewellery from various
sites in the western and northern isles,
9th–11th century. **Viking goldwork**

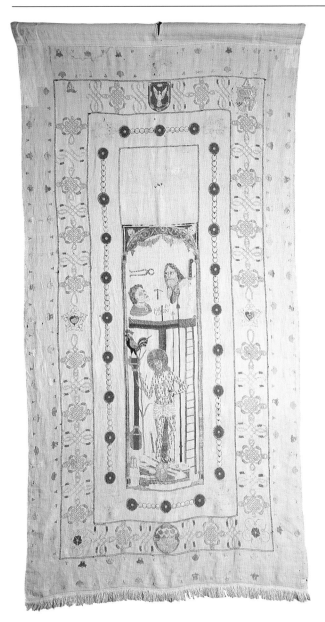

The Fetternear banner, with an
embroidered design of the Image of Pity,
about 1520: the oldest surviving Scottish
embroidery. **Embroidery; Pre-Reformation church furnishings and relics**

Carved Pictish stone from Bullion,
Invergowrie, Angus, 8th–9th century.
Pictish symbols

Cream satin wedding dress, 1914.
Costume

In the detailed study of such material, just as with, for example, items of Oceanic enthnography entirely divorced from original contexts, we often have to apply the research techniques appropriate to fine art objects. Overall form, type and style, and decorative detail are examined and compared with kindred objects, with contemporary manuscript illustrations and the like, and regional or individual characteristics are established by assessing degrees of variation from, for example, the general freemasonry of Christian motifs. This method of approach is demanded by the nature of the material and of the available evidence.

The Middle Ages

From the period before the twelfth century, some knowledge, though scanty, of everyday secular life can be gleaned from a scattering of excavated inhabited sites. These range through hillforts, artificial lake-dwellings or crannogs, Hebridean wheel-houses, and brochs, mostly built with what seems to be a pre-Viking concept of circularity. Although interesting finds were made – weapons, tools, personal adornment that includes gold spiral finger-rings, textile working equipment, dice for gaming, etc – most are of a miscellaneous character. They do not throw as much light as we would like on the life and work of the masses of the time. This element grows increasingly strong however, and a more balanced knowledge begins to be gained of the interactive roles of church and state, rulers and ruled, with the coming of the full Middle Ages. This period saw the foundation of castles and burghs, and of monasteries (always in the country's most fertile spots) that marked the replacing of Celtic Christianity with that of the Romans. The key words are feudalism, church, trade.

Inevitably, the material culture reflects the higher social levels, as well as the products, of foreign craftsmen (usually from the Low Countries, Germany and France). The coming of a new ruling class in the twelfth century and war with England at the end of the thirteenth century inhibited the continuation of native forms of art. The international Romanesque became more acceptable, and Scottish craftsmen began to look more to the Continent, adopting at first and then adapting as time went on.

Out of this period of vast change came many exciting things, many of them dating from the twelfth century. There are stone carvings associated with churches, church furnishings

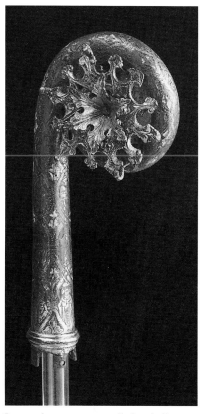

Late 12th-century enamelled and gilt copper crosier found at Whithorn Priory, Wigtownshire.

'Berserker', one of the ivory chessmen carved in the late 12th century found in Lewis.

such as stoups and basins, symbols of church authority such as the Whithorn crosier, bell-shrines such as that from Kilmichael Glassary, crucifixes, and figures of saints. From later in the period can be found woodwork of a fine character, such as the Lincluden choir stalls of about 1470, the Montrose panels and doors of about 1515, the recently acquired Beaton panels of the 1530s, misericords and much else. On these, as on the stone carvings, are motifs such as the Arma Christi, heraldic devices, elements of legendary tales, and figures and faces. The latter include oak statues of saints and bishops, most of which are realistically portrayed, either praying or holding up a book or a symbol of heaven. Even if the figure is dying, receiving extreme unction, as on a fifteenth-century carved stone retable from Edinburgh, the crowd around the bed is still a lively one. Faces are trembling on the brink of portraiture. We have already moved into a concept of death and the afterlife that is far more individualistic than in earlier days, with a seeking after immortality on earth as well as in heaven.

Scotland was remote in itself and the Western Highlands were remoter still, but even there the grave slabs of the fourteenth and fifteenth centuries show realistic figures: Reginald and John of Islay grasping a sword and an axe (about 1380); the late medieval effigy (probably pre-1500) of a civilian who seems to be tying the belt of his tunic; John MacAlister, pastor of Gigha (about 1500–60), with his hands in an attitude of prayer, not slack at his sides as in death.

Surviving medieval textiles also have church associations. The major piece is the Fetternear Banner, an unfinished piece of embroidery dating to about 1520, showing the arms of Bishop Gavin Douglas of Dunkeld, and the figure of Christ with the instruments and symbols of the Passion. There is an altar cloth made of two fourteenth-century copes, probably English, and surely a sign of Scottish thrift. Inevitably, fragments of cloth of gold from the tomb of King Robert the Bruce in Dunfermline Abbey figure in the collections.

There was relaxation as well as religion in the Middle Ages. Amongst a number of fine gaming pieces, the late twelfth-century Lewis chessmen are outstanding. Brooches and rings mark love of finery and symbolize status. Music was a sought-after and revered pastime, leading to the creation of works of art like the Queen Mary (about 1450) and Lamont (about 1500) harps or clarsachs, themselves amongst the earliest in Europe.

Fighting and self-defence are reflected in various ways. Knights

Detail from the Beaton panels, carved in the 1530s, showing the Tree of Jesse.

wore armour and spurs, foot soldiers carried poles and long bows. Daggers were worn in civilian life as well as in battle. Battle axes persisted long in the West Highlands, to judge by representations on monuments, and the same sources show large, two-handed swords or claymores. The two-handed swords popularly linked with Bruce and Wallace in illustrations and descriptions are actually a full century later in date than the War of Independence, but historical mythology does not die easily.

Household vessels were of wood, clay, brass and bronze, with silver and gold being reserved for the upper echelons of society.

Gold bonnet-piece of James V, the first
Scottish coin to bear a date, 1539.

The Finzean Bucket Mill, on the southern edge of Grampian
Region, is the last survivor (now restored) of a long tradition of
the making in the Forest of Birse of wooden vessels for widespread
domestic use. At a time when there were no refrigerators, every
household possessed a great range of storage containers, wooden
tubs and casks, earthenware pigs and mugs. Equipment for
brewing ale was standard in all homes of any scale.

Above and beyond the house, there was as part of the growth of
burghs and the co-ordination of trade, another mark of the kind of
centralizing control that goes with the shaping of a nation. This
was the development of a Scottish coinage. Before the eleventh
century Scotland was already in a monetary common market. The
Vikings brought a new form of culture after AD 800; the zenith of
their power, when they held sway over parts of Scotland and
England, Normandy, Iceland and South Russia, is marked by
wealth symbolized for us by hoards of silver. Two large hoards
found at Skaill and Burray in Orkney contained plain bracelets or
ring-money, armlets and neck-rings, and great brooches of mid-
tenth century date with thistle-shaped terminals that antedate the
adoption of the thistle as the emblem of Scottish nationhood.
Included also are coins, some Anglo-Saxon, some from Samarkand
and Baghdad. A late tenth-century Viking hoard from Iona was
composed almost entirely of coins.

Until the time of David I (1124–53), who had silver pennies
struck at Roxburgh, Berwick, Carlisle and Edinburgh, foreign and
especially English coins circulated in Scotland and internationalism
remained for long a feature in some areas. The man who died in a
peat-bog in Gunnister, Shetland, in the seventeenth century, and
whose clothes are in the National Museums' collections, had a
woollen purse containing a Nijmegen 6-stuiver piece of 1690, an
Overijssel 2-stuiver piece of 1681, and a Swedish øre of 1683.
Even if he was a foreigner, he must still have expected to be able to
use his money. As late as 1806, Dutch and Danish coins were more
common in Lerwick than British money. The Northern Isles may
be a special case and an extreme example, but in general coinage of
other countries remained valid in Scotland long after David I's
mints started operating.

The National Museums' coin cabinet is in a real sense a treasure
chest. It contains the finest series of Scottish coins in existence,
from David I's twelfth-century coinage onwards. The appearance
in the fifteenth century of portraits on coins offers a parallel with
the individualism of sculptures and carvings of the human face in

funerary and other monuments. The first Scottish coin to bear a date, 1539, was James V's bonnet-piece of gold, worth 40 shillings then, showing the king wearing a bonnet. This custom of dating was borrowed from France, and adopted by England some years later. But in spite of the occasional appearance of such status coins, a period of rapid debasement of the coinage and inflation set in, so that by the time of the Union of the Crowns in 1603 a Scottish shilling was worth no more than an English penny, surely a sign that wealth was not then the hallmark of the Scottish nation.

The thrifty Scots had bun-shaped 'pirlie pigs', or piggy banks, from the first half of the sixteenth century, though the English had similar money boxes nearly two centuries earlier.

The early modern period to the beginnings of industrialization

The round date of 1600 may be taken as the beginning of a new era. The Reformation of 1560 was past, and the Presbyterian pulpit had replaced the Catholic altar. The Parton pulpit from Kirkcudbrightshire, dated 1598, bears non-religious carvings and a biblical text suitable for the Bible-reading congregation of a reformed kirk.

The accession in 1603 of James VI to the throne of England led to a widening of the perspectives, aspirations and pretensions of Scottish nobles, certainly affecting the material culture with which they were surrounded. But the to-ing and fro-ing of politics and religion made the country unsettled for over a century. Charles I, who tried to enforce the episcopal system of church government, was anointed with oil by the archbishop at his magnificent coronation in 1633. It was poured from a golden ampulla, now in the national collections. His episcopal aspirations led to the National Covenant of 1638, his defeat in the Bishop's Wars, and the Solemn League and Covenant of 1643 in which Scottish Presbyterians allied themselves with English Parliamentarians after the Civil War had begun in England. Following the restoration of Charles II in 1660 there was a period of persecution of the most rigid Presbyterians, the Covenanters, of whom many relics, including flags, survive. Much of the material culture of the time points straight to the heart of history in which church and state were inextricably entangled.

Whatever its problems, Presbyterianism spawned a crop of

Gold ampulla used at the Scottish coronation of Charles I in 1633.

associated artefacts. Tokens of brass or pewter marked those individuals in parishes, congregations and sects deemed worthy to take part in the Lord's Supper. The earliest dated token is for 1648. Communion vessels, cups and plates of silver or pewter, some showing Dutch influence, can be very fine. And lead beggars' badges of the eighteenth and nineteenth centuries point to one aspect of how the church then carried out parish welfare functions later taken over by local authorities.

Throughout the period there was a feeling of need for the commercialization of agriculture. Efforts were made by the government to facilitate this, through acts passed at various times from 1579 on till those of 1696 relating to lands lying runrig (worked by communities with intermingled strips and patches) and to division of commonties. These enabling acts opened the way for the Lowland proportion of the about 8000 Scottish landowners to begin changing the face of the land, turning old joint farming communities into sets of individual tenant farms with enclosed boundaries.

A technical aspect of the desire for improvement was the increasing adoption of lime as a field fertilizer from the early 1600s, in places where coal was available alongside lime. The lime was burned in oval clamps and later in stone-built kilns. That there was a degree of improvement is suggested by the

Tokens used to admit parishioners to Communion in the Presbyterian Church, 18th and 19th centuries.

Table carpet from Glamis Castle, woven
in the first half of the 17th century.

appearance of new mansions replacing the old towers, with signs
of elegant living that included, amongst other things, tea, coffee
and chocolate services, excellent furniture of which a good
proportion was imported, and in the grandest houses furnishings
like the Glamis Castle table carpet of the first half of the
seventeenth century, itself probably woven in England.

The growth of towns and associated trade and craft production
is a further mark of rising living standards at bourgeois level by
the early 1700s. Glasgow and Stirling craftsmen were producing
their best basket-hilted swords from 1700 to 1745. By the mid-
eighteenth century the appearance of firearms had made armour
obsolete, and the basket hilt replaced the mailed glove as a hand
protector. The Highland stabbing-dagger or dirk went out of
use as a standard weapon after the Jacobite rebellion of 1745.
Numerous highly ornate leather-covered targes survive from
the period. Powder horns of cow horn with pewter or brass
mounts illustrate a revival of Celtic art forms; they fed the
maws of muskets that had distinctive, curving decorated butts
until about 1700.

From the late seventeenth century pistols of metal were being
made in Lowland Scottish towns and villages along the Highland
line, such as Doune in Perthshire. They are outstanding examples
of regionally spread craftsmanship producing local forms. There
are also in the National Museums' collections samples of the
great Highland bagpipes that inspired men to battle and of the

The silver travelling canteen of Prince Charles Edward Stuart: the case and wine beakers were made by Ebenezer Oliphant, Edinburgh, 1740–41.

altogether sweeter Lowland chamber bagpipes that made music in the best houses.

The activities of Prince Charles Edward Stuart marked the last major revolutionary political disturbance in Scotland. Its memory lingers on and related objects are numerous and often of merit. They include the silver travelling canteen with drinking vessels, knives and forks and much else packed ingeniously into a silver case. This is largely the work of an Edinburgh silversmith. It is a further sign of the urban growth that helped to finance both agricultural change and the development of industry, for Scottish silversmiths were active from the late seventeenth century in the major towns and burghs with a well organized

Hammermen's Guild. The Jacobites did not disturb them, though their activities affected the range of arms that people could carry. The degeneration of the Highland dirk into a decorative item, eventually with a fork attached to it in a sheath stuck in the stocking, is a direct aftermath of the Rebellion.

The period of industry and empire

From the mid-eighteenth century development was in a land of peace, and was rapid. In the countryside progress in the Lowland farming areas was marked by new farm buildings, technical advances like James Small's swing plough (1767), Andrew Meikle's threshing mill (1786), Patrick Bell's reaper (1828) and James Smith of Deanston's system of systematic underground drainage of fields (1831) which the spread of tile-works ably supported. For a time farming improvement was so active that Scotland was both a pioneer and leader in Europe.

Industrial development was also proceeding. At first it was water-powered, with a rural base, and before about 1830 concentrated on textiles, linen, cotton and wool. The metal manufactures that became the coal- and steam-based giants of later days were only beginning by this date. Work in the countryside was being diversified by a great range of non-agrarian alternatives, and market forces were becoming dominant.

The comfortable days of Victoria had come upon the country,

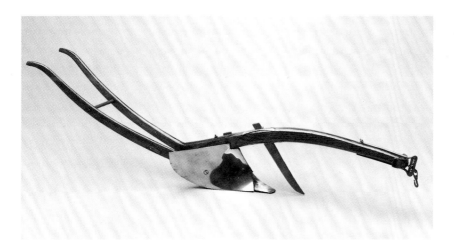

Model of James Small-type plough from the collection that came from the Highland and Agricultural Society.

and people could enjoy a range of leisure activities, quoiting, archery, athletics, bowling, golf, curling, angling, cockfighting and field-sports in general. All of these have left their mark on museum collections in the form of equipment and prizes. At one level, however, the crowding of people in search of work into urbanized and industrialized areas led to a vast extension of tenement building, where cooking was usually done on kitchen ranges from the Carron Company (founded 1759) and other foundries, and in pots and pans with the Carron mark. Municipalization was the mark of the second half of the nineteenth century, with the provision of gas supplies (allowing people longer evenings in which to read the popular press and practise sewing and embroidery), tramcars, hospitals, public baths and washhouses, libraries, museums and art galleries, markets, and so on.

A whole new material culture developed and spread to the masses. No longer were products primarily regional. Instead, there grew up a kind of factory-based mobile culture, in which local blacksmiths were still catering for local tastes, making ornamental bannock spades or oatcake toasters almost as a form of 'folk art'. 'Folk art' is perhaps a concept sparked off in response to the spread of centrally produced and distributed products, a sign of a new romantic or nostalgic attitude to days gone by, and not to be fully equated with the attractive designs that craftsmen applied to distaffs for spinning, the leather of targes, the butts of muskets, the sides of powder horns, the metalwork of lighting devices like peermen and cruisies, etc, in earlier days.

Ornamentation applied to a functional object shows pride in craftsmanship. When an object is ornamented only to be decorative we have moved into a new value system, which may be to a large extent commercial, as in the case of the early nineteenth-century painted wooden boxes for snuff and other purposes, with which museum and private collections teem. Even the tartan that outsiders see as a mark of Scotland, and all the paraphernalia of Highland dress that go with it, grew in great degree out of Sir Walter Scott's romantic view of history and the support given to it by George IV on his kilt-clad visit to Edinburgh in 1822.

By the mid-nineteenth century documentation of material culture through the written word was running at a level never known before, and was indeed becoming systematized, as the science of folklore (the word was invented by a Scot, W J Thoms,

White-painted oak bookcase designed by
Charles Rennie Mackintosh for Dunglass
Castle, Dunbartonshire, 1900.

in 1846) evolved from antiquarianism. Though at first applied to customs, beliefs, tales and other aspects of spiritual culture, it had come to embrace material culture also by the end of the century, especially in seeking for primitive survivals, the past in the present, as steps marking man's civilized progress, or lack of it. Modern material culture brought into focus a subconsciously patronizing view of the past, of which the phenomenon of folk art is part. Nevertheless, it was an attitude that has filled our museums with good things, and we should be grateful.

About the same time too a major new means of recording appeared: that of photography. Once cheap, commercial cameras had become generally available, there was no spot in the land, no family group, no festival occasion, that could not be snapped for posterity. Only recently, however, have museum curators and others come to realize the importance of collecting such pictures for their value in helping to interpret the material culture and human activities – or stilted poses – that they preserve.

The present day

In this modern world, when the twentieth century is far from new, museums are faced with a great problem: how to cope with the massive technology of industrialization on the one hand, and with the countless multitudes of new products made in new materials that come and go year by year, on the other?

Twentieth-century collecting is a key phrase in current museum thought. It covers two interrelated concepts, the first concerned with material that is excellent in its own right, that sets fashions in taste and design, and that may itself spark off a school. The work of Charles Rennie Mackintosh is an example. The second relates to the material of everyday life, the bakelite, plastic, veneered and generally mass-produced needs that in themselves, like the casings

Yamaha TZR 250 motorcycle, 1988. *(The Scotsman Publications Ltd)*

of early radios, or wartime utility furniture, or the emancipated clothes of women in the 1920s and '30s, are pieces of period design that may point to concepts and events of world significance, such as the radio and the two World Wars.

The material culture reflecting the social life of today probably needs to be selectively preserved in contextualized groupings to give it significance for the future, but much of it is no longer essentially linked to any part of Scotland, or to Scotland as a whole, or even to Britain. Museum concern with how to handle this problem will not stop research into the things we used in past years. There are indeed huge gaps to be filled, for example through computerized examination of the lists of goods in wills, of which the Scottish Record Office holds a rich store from the sixteenth century onwards. Such work will go on, just as scientific techniques will continue to make more precise and far reaching our knowledge of prehistoric periods.

In their collections of material culture museums have the task of representing the past, present and future, and in our case, of Scotland in particular. At every period, Scotland has been part of Europe. Now, we are part of the whole world, in what we wear, in what we eat, and in all that lies around us.

THE
SCOTTISH
COLLECTIONS

This section is a compendium of information on the Scottish material in the National Museums of Scotland. The Scottish collections are linked with all aspects of Scottish life and culture. They are a vast archive of evidence, silent witnesses to momentous events and humble domesticity, to invention and discovery, to energy and creativity, to toil and leisure.

Their nature also reflects the history of the Museums themselves and the interests and attitudes of different times and different individuals. They cover many disciplines and subjects, and they take their place alongside the Museums' international collections, which contain material from all over the world.

Each of the following entries helps to fill in the broad picture of 'the wealth of a nation' in the National Museums. Many collections that contain Scottish material are not in themselves specifically Scottish. Scotland has always had vigorous and productive contacts with the rest of the world, and science and learning foster these. But some material is distinctively, if not uniquely, Scottish. The total effect indicates both a Scottish identity and the place of Scotland on a wider stage.

Different disciplines require different approaches. Natural history, for example, is covered by a single entry, as it is not helpful to group species found in Scotland under separate headings. Many of the Museums' collections are so extensive each could command a volume to itself, so in some areas, notably archaeology, entries focus on significant aspects.

The entries are arranged in alphabetical order, cross-referenced and indexed. It is hoped that this will help readers to find information easily. Readers who wish to know more are encouraged to make use of the reading list, to make contact with the Museums, and especially to visit the displays.

Joseph Anderson and George Black in the National Museum of Antiquities at the Royal Institution, 1890, showing some of the most valued objects in the collections.

The collections are located in many different buildings, some of which have their own identity as separate museums. Exhibition space is at a premium, and so many objects and specimens cannot be displayed. Others, collected for research purposes, are not intended for display. The museums that make up the National Museums of Scotland can be found on the map on page 197. Curatorial staff are based mainly in the two Royal Museum of Scotland buildings in Chambers Street and Queen Street, Edinburgh. Readers will also find, on page 198, a list of contributors to this volume.

The old Gas Showrooms at Biggar Gasworks Museum.

A selection of some of the National Museums' most valued objects, including Charles I's coronation ampulla and jewellery of Mary, Queen of Scots. **Banknotes; Coins; Medieval and Renaissance Jewellery; Sports and games; Viking goldwork**

Roman bronze bowls from Helmsdale, Sutherland, 1st–2nd century AD. **Roman bronze tableware**

MALCOLM McPHERSON
corporal *in the Highland Regiment who was Shot in the Tower July the 18.ᵗʰ 1743 for desertion.* Sold by John Bowles at ȳ BlackHorse in Cornhil.

Corporal Malcolm McPherson of the 43rd Highland Regiment, 1740s. **Military Uniform**

Telangium affine (L & H), a characteristic Carboniferous Oil Shale (340 million years ago) seed fern from Burdiehouse, Edinburgh. The Museums have the specimens on which Hugh Miller based his excellent 1857 restoration of this plant. **Plants: fossil**

Barr and Stroud motorcycle engine, about 1923, made in Glasgow, and a copper electric kettle, about 1914, made by GEC. **Public utilities; Transport**

Agates
see Semi-precious stones

Agriculture
see Farming and fishing; Man and beast

Amphibians: fossil

Amphibians are a class of backboned animals which often live on land as adults, but must return to water to lay their eggs. The frogs and newts living today are survivors of a group far more diverse in the past than now. Some extinct relatives reached the size of large crocodiles. Others were eel-like and limbless, or had strange horned skulls. We can recognize their bones in rocks of various parts of the world and trace their story back to a heyday in the coal swamps about 310 million years ago (Ma).

At that time amphibians were very diverse and had already given rise to reptiles (see **Reptiles: fossil**). All known coal-swamp amphibians are from Europe and North America, then enjoying a tropical climate, and the coal-mines of southern Scotland have produced a good share of them. The Museums' fine collection was built up gradually, through efforts of such little-known collectors as the 19th-century miner, Joseph Blair (see **Fossils**).

Fossil amphibians were always rarer than other backboned animals, even while flourishing in the coal swamps. However, in the earlier Carboniferous (360–320 Ma) they were even rarer, known only from about a dozen localities in the Midland Valley of Scotland and a further half dozen in North America and Europe. Because of its palaeogeography and geology Scotland thus yields more amphibians from this early period than the rest of the world combined. A large proportion of them, including many type specimens (see **Fossils**), are in the Scottish national collection, which is of international significance.

Despite this relative wealth we have only tantalizing glimpses of some ancestral lines giving rise to the varied animals of coal-swamp times, and until recently all known examples were water-dwellers. In 1984 a new locality was discovered by commercial collector Stan Wood, at East Kirkton, West Lothian, in unusual volcanic hot-spring rocks of about 340 Ma. The amphibians are all new to science. They include the earliest known land-dwelling members of several groups and a limbless burrower, and many specimens have recently been acquired for the Museums. The number of animals of this period known from complete skeletons seems likely to double (from seven)!

In addition to amphibians, there are at East Kirkton fossil scorpions, millipedes, a harvestman spider, eurypterids (see **Eurypterids**) and many kinds of land plants (see **Plant: fossil**). This exciting discovery provides a unique view of life on land at that remote time. The Museums are excavating the site and co-ordinating the work of an international team of researchers.

Almost complete skeleton of an *Eoherpeton*-like anthracosaur in the East Kirkton Limestone, 340 million years old (180 mm long as preserved).

Restoration of *Eoherpeton*. (*Hunterian Museum, University of Glasgow* Modern Geology)

Amulets
see Charms and amulets

Animal husbandry
see Man and beast

Animals
see Natural History Collections

Cast-iron drinking fountain and canopy
by Walter Macfarlane & Co, Glasgow,
about 1880. *(Crowther of Syon Lodge Ltd)*

Applied mathematics
see also **History of physical science**

In the 17th century many associated the name of John Napier of Merchiston with the simple calculating rods, commonly called 'Napier's Bones' – as sets were often made from ivory. There are a number of sets held by the National Museums. A set on cylinders, after Gaspar Schott's design of about 1660, is probably Scottish, dating from about 1700. The adding machine called 'Rotula Arithmetica' for which George Brown of Kilmaurs was granted a patent by the Privy Council in 1698, is represented by two complete and two incomplete examples. The naïvety of the device reflects the low level of numeracy in Scotland at the time.

It was two Englishmen, Edmund Gunter and William Oughtred, who demonstrated the instrumental application of Napier's logarithms (see **History of physical science**). The Gunter sector and the Gunter rule remained standard calculating devices for navigation and in other practical applications of trigonometry for two and a half centuries from their publication in 1623. There are examples in the collections, but none is of Scottish origin. There is, however, an Edinburgh-made example, of about 1650, of Oughtred's 1632 design for a circular logarithmic slide rule.

By the 18th century the logarithmic slide rule, typically in the linear form, was widely used, but it was made with scales specially laid out to assist routine calculations peculiar to specialist trades. There are only a handful of peculiarly Scottish slide rules, those used in hydrometry. Here the rule was used in place of a book of tables to normalize observations to a standard temperature. There are examples associated with the hydrometer designed by Thomas Thomson and used in the early 19th century by the Scottish Excise to ascertain the strength of spirits. Others are linked with the aerometrical beads patented by Isobel Lovi of Edinburgh in 1805, and used to measure the density of liquids. Paradoxically, the scales on such rules are not logarithmic!

Among the draughting instruments in the collection are examples of the 'eidograph'. This was a radically improved version of the pantograph, and was used to make precision copies, enlargements and reductions of technical drawings. The published design dates from 1824 and was the work of William Wallace, Professor of Mathematics in the University of Edinburgh. There are examples in the collection used by the Edinburgh cartographic business of John Bartholomew. There is also an example of the 1821

'apograph' designed for similar purposes by the Ayrshire inventor Andrew Smith.

Architectural ironwork
see also **Domestic metalwork**

Smithing as a craft has always had an important place in Scottish society, linked in earlier centuries to the need for swords, spears and armour in warfare and to the domestic use of pots and girdles. Ironwork also played a defensive role, and its strength made its use vital in the production of *yetts*, massive hinged gates of interlacing iron bars which were a feature of Scottish medieval tower houses. There are examples of these in the National Museums.

The advent of a more generally settled period in Scotland's history in the late 17th and early 18th centuries resulted in a move away from the purely utilitarian use of wrought iron, and smiths began to develop more decorative skills. Scottish ironwork from this period has a strong, robust style and a character and charm of its own, ideally suited both to Scotland's architecture and to her changeable climate. Traquair House near Innerleithen has fine examples of late 17th-century work decorated with botanical themes such as lilies and thistles. This use of natural forms was an interesting feature of early decorative smithwork.

In the 18th century the skills of the smith were employed by architects, many of whom used imaginative ironwork as an integral part of their schemes. However, developments in the ironfounding industry in the late 18th and early 19th century and the subsequent introduction and relative cheapness of cast iron significantly reduced the demand for the more expensive wrought iron, and cast iron became the preferred choice for architectural features.

The Great Exhibition of 1851, and later international exhibitions, including one in Edinburgh and two in Glasgow, used cast iron extensively in their buildings. The manufacturers also displayed their wares in countless decorative and functional variations. Many buildings incorporated cast iron in their structure, including the Royal Museum of Scotland in Chambers Street, Edinburgh, whose main hall is one of the most impressive examples of iron and glass construction in Scotland.

The considerable demand for cast iron was supplied by iron foundries such as Macfarlane's 'Saracen' Ironworks, Glasgow. A fine example of this firm's work is the late 19th-century cast-iron drinking fountain and decorative canopy in the Museums' collections.

The early 20th century saw a renewed interest in wrought iron, which was revived by architects such as Sir Robert Lorimer, who greatly encouraged the revitalization of Scottish vernacular and Renaissance traditions. Lorimer worked closely with the Edinburgh smithing firm of Thomas Hadden, examples of whose work can be seen in the screens in the Thistle Chapel in St Giles Cathedral, Edinburgh, and in the gates and steel casket of the National War Memorial on Edinburgh Castle rock. The National Museums have the iron test pieces for the figures on the casket.

Following the Second World War the wrought-iron industry again went into decline, not least because of the changes in architectural styles and tastes. The move towards functionalism resulted in a dearth of commissions for blacksmiths, and firms such as Hadden's ceased production.

Armlets
see **Massive and snake armlets**

Astronomy, navigation and surveying
see also **History of physical science**

Astronomy was the first of the sciences to require specialist instruments to observe, measure and compute. A 15th-century European astrolabe used by the cartographer Robert Gordon of Straloch in the 17th century is the earliest Scottish-related item in the collections. The three-foot radius astronomical quadrant of about 1710, from the Natural Philosophy Collections of the University of Edinburgh, is of particular interest. It may be identified as that presented by Lord Hope to the Philosophical Society of Edinburgh in 1737. It is London made, probably by John Rowley.

A vertical orrery by John Miller of Edinburgh is also from the University Natural Philosophy Collections. This splendid piece of equipment shows the relative motions of the planets in the solar system. It was specifically designed for classroom demonstrations, and is quite different from the conventional horizontal table orreries of the period. There is a small 'portable observatory', also by John Miller – a remarkably versatile mounted telescope which could be used to undertake almost every form of astronomical measurement.

There are a number of reflecting telescopes by James Short, including one used by Professor Colin Maclaurin. Few of the later Scottish telescopes have known provenance, and most are typical trade goods, used for amateur stargazing. Technically interesting are 19th century reflectors made by James Veitch of Inchbonny, and in Kilmarnock by the textile engineer Thomas Morton.

By the 19th century, the Scottish workshops were able

Showroom of Walter Macfarlane & Co's Saracen Foundry, Glasgow, about 1885.

Orrery made after 1752 by G Jamieson
the younger, Hamilton, after the design
of James Fergusson; pocket terrestrial
globe and case by John Miller,
Edinburgh, after 1793.

to produce the standard equipment for topographical surveys. There is a full range of these instruments. A typical mine surveyor's compass by Adie of Edinburgh, has an inscription indicating that it was presented to Andrew Adamson, overseer at Halbeath Colliery, in 1830. More prosaic are examples of the drainage level made to the design registered by T R Gardner of Glasgow in 1850.

With the exception of the various Thomson pattern marine compasses made by White of Glasgow in the later 19th century, navigating equipment made in Scotland is to typical London design – indeed many 19th-century sextants, ostensibly of Scottish origin, were imported from London and retailed. Of rather more interest is a small box sextant made by Adie of Edinburgh, inscribed to indicate that it was used by Sir Thomas Makdougall Brisbane to regulate the time of the army during the Peninsular War.

Axes
see Maces, battleaxes and axe hammers

Bagpipes

The bagpipe is a musical instrument whose history marches with the evolution and progress of civilization. There have been many types of bagpipes over the centuries and the National Museums have not only a representative collection of the many types of British and European bagpipe but also a rare example of its primitive relative, the hornpipe.

In certain respects Scotland has made the bagpipe very much her own. It developed its own distinctive size, style and pitch, and took on an unusual role of intensive service to the aristocracy and the army. It has acquired a vast

Dancing to the music of a street piper
playing a set of bellows bagpipes: etching
by Walter Geikie, about 1830.

traditional and written repertoire, special features of playing technique, an ancient word notation, and a considerable corpus of musical works in long extended forms of a type unique in Europe.

The bagpipe in Europe was in decline by the 16th and 17th centuries and piping as an art form was tending to be identified as the province of village musicians and shepherds in the hills. At this period piping was enjoying a popularity in Scotland, not only in the Lowlands where the burghs aspired to have musicians in the same way as king and court, but also increasingly in the Highlands where leaders adopted the instrument in the place of the harp as the ideal medium for praise and inspiration (see **Harps**). It was in this heroic society of Gaelic Scotland that *piobaireachd* or *ceòl mór* evolved as such a sophisticated art form.

The collection of British bagpipes in the National Museums takes several distinctive forms. The most familiar is the strident Highland bagpipe, which has a chanter playing at a relatively high pitch and a set of three drones providing powerful and sustained harmonics. The Lowland or Border bagpipe, which was the favoured instrument of burgh pipers, has the same chanter and tuning arrangement as the Highland bagpipe, carries the three drones in a common stock, and has usually been inflated by bellows. Small pipes also using bellows were once commonly played as a domestic instrument in Scotland but survive vigorously and in a more sophisticated form in Northumberland.

Another type of bagpipe which is well represented in the Museums is the older relative of the Irish *uillean* bagpipe. It was developed in the 18th century for chamber orchestra performance in an era when the arcadian and pastoral were in vogue. The instrument developed a wider melodic range in line with contemporary wind instrumentation and also 'regulators' which sounded a range of extra chords to augment the harmonics of two, three or more drones.

As the bagpipe was supplanted in the vernacular tradition by other musical instruments such as the Jew's harp, the fiddle and the accordion, it is perhaps something of a miracle that it has survived with such vigour as a cultural symbol of Scottish nationality.

Banknotes
see also **Coins; Trade tokens**

In 1707 the Act of Union abolished Scotland's national coinage, but at the same time a new form of currency emerged. Paper promissory notes were originally introduced by the first Scottish bank, the Bank of Scotland, founded in 1695. Due to the inherent strength of the Scottish banking system, which was based mainly on a relatively few large 'public' banks operating a branch system, these notes were popular with the public. Unlike early English notes, they were actually preferred to coins, a situation not unheard of today! Consequently, over the past three centuries a great deal of care and attention has been lavished on their design and production, mainly for security reasons but also out of a sense of corporate pride.

This has led to a large number of types and designs of note and the National Museums' collection attempts to cover this range as comprehensively as possible, forming a typological reference tool.

The earliest notes had relatively simple designs printed on one side only and relying on the complexity of their script to prevent forgery. A Bank of Scotland note of 1723 shows that these early notes were cut from a counterfoil book, rather like modern cheques, and were signed and dated by hand.

As banking developed and more banks were founded (the Royal Bank of Scotland opened in 1727, followed by what became the British Linen Bank in 1746) notes became more complicated. Elaborate decorative scenes were introduced, often taken from the bank's arms, or, as in the case of the 1848 series of Commercial Bank of Scotland notes, from the architecture of their head office.

Around 1860 advances in photography prompted the banks to introduce two-colour printing. The use of certain colours, particularly blue and red, made photographic forgery difficult as they did not reproduce well on negatives of the day. Throughout the 19th and 20th centuries banks continued to develop their note designs, keeping up with technical innovations. Printing on the back of the notes as an additional security measure, for example, was introduced in Scotland many years before it appeared in England.

By the early 20th century Scottish notes were recognized as masterpieces of the art. Despite many changes in banking practice, these notes have remained immensely popular right up to the present day, although the current development of 'plastic' money may finally herald their death knell.

Bank of Scotland banknote for £12 Scots or £1 sterling, 1723.

Reverse of Commercial Bank of Scotland banknote for £1, 1849: engraved by W H Lizars, Edinburgh and showing revenue stamp.

Brooches
see **Heart brooches; Pseudo-penannular brooches; Ring brooches**

Battleaxes
see **Maces, battleaxes and axe hammers**

Bog costume
see **Costume**

Bronze age dagger graves

This distinctive group of bronze age burials is represented by 18 Scottish examples, of which eight cluster around the coast of Fife and Angus. They are thought to fall within the period from about 1950 BC to 1600 BC, and are comparable with dagger graves from elsewhere in Britain and Ireland (of which the most famous are in Wessex). Eleven of the 18 Scottish daggers are in the collections.

These graves are distinguished not only by the presence of a bronze dagger, but also by other features which suggest that the interred individual was accorded special status. Firstly, the stone cists in which all but one of the Scottish daggers were found tend to be larger than other contemporary cists, and some have the added elaboration of massive capstones and/or clay luting to seal the gaps between the stones. Secondly, two of the cists were constructed for full-length rather than crouched burials, which were commoner at the time. Thirdly, the cairns which cover eight of the cists are almost all remarkably large: Carlochan cairn, for example, is reputed to have been the largest in Galloway. Finally, in two cases (Masterton, Fife and Bishopmill, Moray), remains of oxhide skins were found in the cists.

Where information on the age and sex of the individual is available, the evidence consistently suggests that this special treatment was reserved for men in their fifties. These men would have been considered old by the standards of the time, and were evidently respected as elders.

The daggers themselves are usually represented only by their bronze blade, the organic hilt and sheath having decayed away. However, complete or fragmentary hilts have survived in six cases: five are certainly of horn, and of these the hilt from Ashgrove, Fife, was constructed with two horn plates surrounding a central wooden plate. The hilts were attached to the blade by rivets. Pommels of whale ivory (from Ashgrove) and gold-bound wood (from Blackwaterfoot, Arran, Collessie, Fife, and Skateraw, East Lothian) underline the fact that these daggers were prestige items.

Five fragmentary sheaths of animal skin survive, and two of these have a wooden backing. The Kirkcaldy sheath is plain, with a side seam, but the Ashgrove sheath had sewn ribs running lengthwise.

The blades range from 4 in (10.5 cm) to nearly 10 in (25 cm) in length; some are plain, with a simple bevelled edge, whilst others have one to three ribs running vertically or in a V-shape. Three have dot-punched decoration.

Bronze dagger and gold hilt-band from Blackwaterfoot, Arran, 1950–1600 BC. The original handle has not survived.

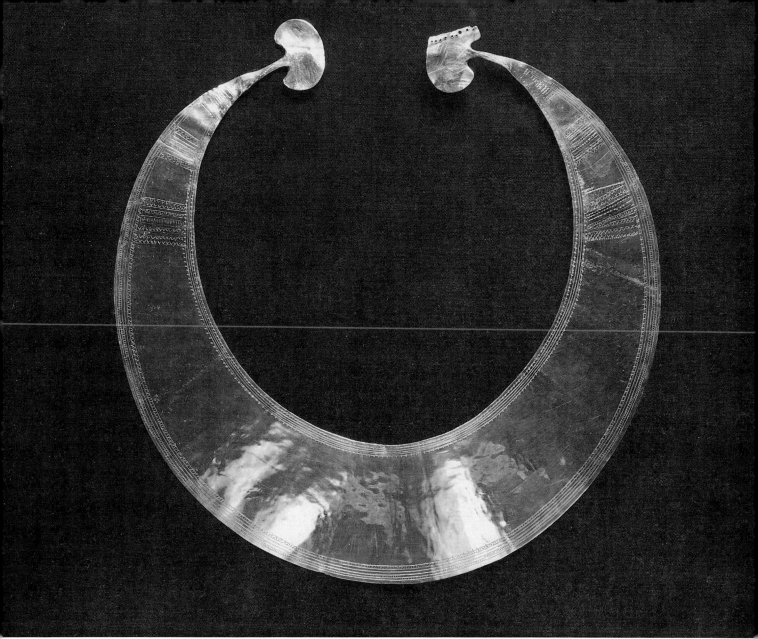

Lunula (collar) from Auchentaggart,
Dumfriesshire, made from sheet gold
with incised decoration, about 2000 BC.

The source of the raw materials and the place of manufacture remain uncertain, but both could be within
Scotland. Analysis of the gold hilt bands suggests a distinctive Scottish gold source, whose material also appears
to have been used for a comparable hilt-band from Topped
Mountain, Co. Fermanagh, and for the gold discs from the
Knowes of Trotty, Orkney (see **Bronze age goldwork**).

Bronze age goldwork

Gold ranks alongside copper as the earliest metal to have
been used in Britain and Ireland. The earliest Scottish
goldwork, which dates from between 2200 BC and 1600 BC,
consists of sheet gold ornaments: basket-shaped earrings,

lunulae (crescent-shaped collars), discs, dagger hilt-bands
(see **Bronze age dagger graves**) and caps for rivets
of archers' wristguards. All would have been status symbols, and all display a remarkable degree of skill in
their manufacture.

The enigmatic discs from the Knowes of Trotty, Orkney
may have been attached to shallow cone-shaped buttons;
their decoration resembles that of contemporary 'Food
Vessel'-style pottery. A similar translation of design
elements applies to lunulae and 'Beaker'-style pottery.

The craft of goldworking may have been introduced to
Scotland from Ireland, and continuing Irish connections
are suggested by the presence of lunulae in Scotland
(lunulae are thought to have originated in Ireland) and the

hilt-band from Topped Mountain, Co. Fermanagh (which is apparently made from Scottish gold). Analysis of the Knowes of Trotty discs and the Scottish hilt-bands suggests that these pieces were probably made from Scottish gold, identical to that used for the Topped Mountain hilt-band.

Goldwork in Scotland from the period 1600 BC to 900 BC is characterized by the use of cast, rather than sheet gold. The items in question comprise two penannular bracelets and three penannular rings from Duff House, Banff; three documented bar torcs (neck- or arm-rings made from a twisted bar of gold); and six ribbon torcs (similar, but made from a gold strip). At least 44 more ribbon torcs are known to have existed; these were melted down or lost soon after their discovery. The Duff House bracelets, the bar torcs and some of the ribbon torcs may well have been imported from Ireland.

Late bronze age goldwork demonstrates technological continuity from the preceding period (in that most pieces are cast), and continuity of links with Ireland. This link is particularly clear in the penannular bracelets with expanded ends, which cluster in the south-west and central belt and which may, in some cases, represent actual Irish imports.

Other late bronze age gold artefacts comprise another variant of the penannular bracelet (the so-called 'Covesea' type, with outwardly-pointing expanding ends), 'dress fasteners' (bracelet-sized penannular rings with cup-shaped ends – another possible Irish import), 'lock rings', and a unique corrugated band of bracelet size from the Easter Ross hoard. This is the largest surviving late bronze age hoard, and also includes 'dress fasteners' and penannular brooches. The majority of the Scottish bronze age gold artefacts are housed in the National Museums.

Bronze age sheet metalwork

Before about 800 BC the use of sheet – as opposed to cast – bronze in Scotland is attested by only a handful of objects, all items of personal adornment. However, during the 8th century, a flourishing sheet-bronze industry existed in Scotland, producing large items of ceremonial and ritual function: cauldrons, 'buckets' and shields. These items, together with contemporary weaponry and ornaments of cast bronze and gold, suggest a period in which various forms of ostentatious display – feasting, ritualized combat, conspicuous acts of worship and the wearing of 'flashy' jewellery – were the main way in which the élite expressed their status.

The ultimate origins of sheet-bronze cauldrons lie in the eastern Mediterranean. The idea of using them spread to western Europe through trading around 800 BC. The cauldron from Darnhall, Peeblesshire, is made from three sheets, riveted together. The bronze is thickest at the base of the vessel, and there were originally two suspension rings at the rim. The cauldron weighs over $5\frac{1}{2}$ lb (2.5 kg), has a maximum circumference of nearly 2.2 yd (2 m), and is almost 16 in (40 cm) high. It could have accommodated a substantial amount of meat, and may well have been used in association with a cast-bronze flesh fork such as the one from the Inveraray Estates.

The inelegantly-named 'buckets' also have an exotic origin, in Kurdish artefacts; the idea of their use spread across Europe from 800 BC onwards, and similar examples can be found in the Etruscan civilization of northern Italy. The technology used for their production in Scotland shares many features with cauldron manufacture, such as the use of wire to strengthen the rim. The example from Flanders Moss, Perthshire, illustrates this feature well. 'Buckets' were probably used to contain alcoholic beverages, and they complement cauldrons as items connected with feasting. A sheet-bronze bowl from Adabrock, Lewis, resembles a squatter version of a bucket, and was probably used for the same purpose.

Bronze shield, 700–600 BC, found at Yetholm, Roxburghshire: such shields were status symbols rather than functional.

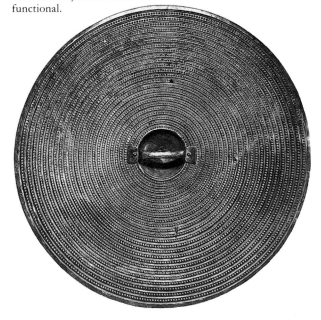

'Stirling head', about 1540: carved wood medallion allegedly representing Margaret Tudor, from a ceiling in the palace, Stirling Castle.

Large and elaborately decorated shields, which were used only for display, are found in contexts which suggest ritual burial. Three Scottish hoards are known: from Yetholm, Roxburghshire, Beith, Ayrshire, and Auchmaleddie, Aberdeenshire. The five or six shields from Beith were found in a bog, placed in a circle. Shields represent a *tour de force* of the sheet bronzesmith's art. They are beaten out from a circular ingot of bronze to a diameter of some 17 to 28 in (45 to 70 cm) and then decorated with ribs and bosses, raised from the back of the shield.

Also contemporary with such items is the cast-bronze trumpet from Innermessan, Wigtownshire, which could have been used to complement any of the activities mentioned above.

Carved and painted woodwork of the 16th and 17th centuries

There are practically no complete schemes of decoration dating from the 16th and 17th centuries. The National Museums have fortunately collected various examples of panels and doors and pieces of painted ceilings.

The earliest surviving wood carvings come from churches. These include the choir stalls of the late 15th century from Lincluden Collegiate Church, near Dumfries and decorative pieces from the choir of St Nicholas Church in Aberdeen. These latter pieces, late Gothic in style, are the work of a Scottish wright, John Fendour, who was contracted to do the work in 1507. The bosses and ribs of

wooden ceilings in domestic and religious buildings, and sometimes the panelling which clad the walls of the better appointed rooms, were also carved. Heraldic and religious decoration figures prominently in such schemes.

The culmination of this Scottish gothic style of wood carving is the Beaton Panels, commissioned by Cardinal David Beaton in the 1530s for one of his residences. In addition to large floral and heraldic panels they include a Tree of Jesse and an Annunciation copied from a French printed Book of Hours.

In the 1530s a new style of wood carving was introduced into Scotland. The earliest and best examples come from the royal palace built in Stirling Castle by James V and they are obviously the work of French or foreign-trained craftsmen. This Renaissance style has medallion panels containing busts, some of classical figures and some of men and women in contemporary costume, as well as acanthus, strapwork, vases and grotesques, and other motifs inspired or derived from Italian art. The ceiling of the presence chamber was closely set with large circular panels with busts or dancing putti, the so-called 'Stirling Heads'. The walls of some of the chambers were covered with new-style panelling. Examples of this style come from other royal residences or important houses, including one which used to stand in Blythe's Close in Edinburgh, allegedly occupied at one time by James V's widow, Mary of Guise.

Not all carved woodwork of the period aspires to the sophistication of that from the royal palaces. There were

Figures in contemporary costume carved
on panels from a bed from Threave
Castle, late 16th century.

surfaces of walls and ceilings were also often decoratively painted. From Wester Livilands House near Stirling comes a screen with a series of the Sibyls dating to 1629. A rare 15th-century survival is the planks from the barrel-vaulted roof of the burial aisle at Guthrie Church with a depiction of the Last Judgement. Such barrel ceilings were to be found in early 17th-century houses. A series of paintings of religious and other subjects from a ceiling in Dean House near Edinburgh is notable. The decoration of a painted ceiling was usually applied directly to the joists and underside of planks of the floor above, such as the very fine example from Rossend Castle in Fife, probably done about 1617.

Carved stone balls

Nearly 400 examples of these enigmatic stone balls are known, about half of which are in the National Museums. All but five come from Scotland: three from northern England, one from Ireland and one from Norway. Within Scotland the majority have been found in the area between the River Tay and the Moray Firth, particularly in the rich agricultural lands east of the Grampians.

There is no immediately obvious explanation of their use but there have been a number of interpretations. It has been suggested that they were used as weapons or in games, and that they may even have formed part of simple weighing machines. All of these ideas, and the many others proposed, have significant drawbacks of one kind or another. The most widely-accepted view today is that they were symbols of authority used on ceremonial occasions. A modern analogy might be the orb held by the monarch during the coronation service.

The balls are remarkably uniform in overall size with all but 12 having diameters close to $2\frac{1}{2}$ in (7 cm); the largest diameter is only $4\frac{1}{2}$ in (11.4 cm). This uniformity is not matched by the decorative treatments given to the balls although almost half have six knobs of one form or another. The smallest number of knobs is three and the largest 160. Some of the most outstanding balls are decorated with spirals and other curved motifs. This is the case with the finest example of all, from Towie, Aberdeenshire, where the quality of the craftsmanship suggests that it was carved with a copper or bronze tool.

Apart from the examples from Skara Brae on Orkney, none of the balls has been found in circumstances that help to determine their date. Indeed, their distribution pattern is so similar to that of Pictish sculptured stones (see **Pictish symbols**) that they were once thought to be

local craftsmen who produced carvings in a more native and often very lively idiom, work such as the late 16th-century pieces said to be from a bed from Threave Castle, Kirkcudbrightshire, remodelled into a bookcase. These have small figures in contemporary costume. A door dated 1600 from Amisfield Castle, Dumfriesshire, shows Samson rending the jaws of a lion.

Although there is little trace of it now, much of this woodwork was originally brightly painted. The flat

Stone ball from Towie, Aberdeenshire,
carved possibly with a metal blade,
about 2500 BC.

'powers'. Just as significant were their supposed healing properties. Rock crystal was thought to hold strong healing powers, particularly for cattle diseases. The Museums have a number of rock crystal balls and pieces, many mounted in silver. Amongst the most notable are the Glenorchy charmstone and the charm of the Stewarts of Ardsheal. These charms were usually dipped into the cattle's drinking water. Other cures for cattle include 'adder stones', small beads of vitreous paste thought to have been discarded by adders, which were again dipped in water and used for snake bites.

Further 'natural' charms held in the Museums include Barbeck's Bone, from Argyllshire, made of a slab of elephant ivory and celebrated as a cure for madness; a goose's thrapple from Kirkcudbright bent into a ring shape and filled with duck shot; a charm against whooping cough; and four amber beads regarded by the Macdonalds of Glencoe as a cure for blindness.

Charms also came in written form and those for toothache were carried on the person of the sufferer. The

post-Roman objects. The finds from Skara Brae, together with the close similarity between some of the decorative motifs and those on stones built into the large communal tombs of the earliest agricultural communities, suggest that the balls were made in the third millennium BC.

Charms and amulets
see also **Heart brooches**

The use of charms and amulets to ward off evil spirits or effect cures in animals and humans has been practised in Scotland since earliest times. Examples of protective charms held in the Museums include rowan crosses, two small pieces of rowan twig tied together with red wool or thread to form a cross. This cross was regarded as a powerful charm against witches and evil in general, when placed in the lining of clothing. The collections contain a calf's heart stuck with pins, also thought to ward off evil. Although its function is not entirely clear, it was thought that if the heart of an animal was slowly roasted at a fire and pins stuck into it, this would force a witch to release animal or human victims from her spell.

The protective role of charms and amulets, while important in Scottish folklore, was only one aspect of their

Silver-mounted crystal healing charm of
the Stewarts of Ardsheal.

Museums have a written charm which was sold in 1855 by Kate McAulay from Lochcarron, Ross-shire.

Throughout the West Highlands and Islands various seeds were greatly prized. The seeds, which were carried across the Atlantic by the Gulf Stream and washed up on the west coast, were used principally for the alleviation of labour pains. The Museums' example was greatly valued in the Western Isles by the local midwives.

Chemical apparatus

From the earliest days chemists developed a distinctive *batterie de cuisine* for practising their processes. Exotic-sounding vessels such as aludels, alembics and pelicans were used alongside those raided from the ordinary kitchen. Joseph Black, professor of chemistry at Edinburgh University from 1766–99, refers to the use of teacups, beer glasses and 'a cylindrical glass-vessel such as confectioners have in their shops'.

Examples of both simple and sophisticated chemical apparatus of the 18th and 19th centuries are in the National Museums of Scotland which possess one of the most significant collections of its kind. In 1858 the new professor at Edinburgh, Lyon Playfair, offered antiquated apparatus to George Wilson, the first director of the Industrial Museum of Scotland, who had strong interests in the history of science. The apparatus (now known as the Playfair Collection) was connected with the golden age of Edinburgh chemistry when students flocked in from England, continental Europe and North America to attend the lectures of William Cullen (professor from 1755–1766), Black, and Thomas Charles Hope (professor from 1795–1843).

Most of the apparatus can be associated with the experiments demonstrated to students though some might have been used in Black's discovery of carbon dioxide in the mid-1750s. One item predates Cullen: a unique early double-barrelled air pump to a design of 1717.

There were no specialist chemical-instrument makers in Scotland until well into the 19th century. But Black does seem to have stimulated a local bottleworks to produce his chemical glassware. This was the Edinburgh and Leith Glasshouse Company which probably made the 24 pieces of elegant green glassware in the Playfair Collection. These range from simple flasks and cucurbits (shaped like gourds) to a long-necked Florentine flask, an alembic and three retorts (all used in distillation processes).

In the early 19th century chemical apparatus became more sophisticated and demonstrations a *tour de force*. Hope demonstrated spectacular experiments at popular

Two glass retorts from the Playfair Collection.

18th-century balance, reputedly used by Joseph Black, from the Playfair Collection.

balance can therefore be seen as representing a turning point: the mystical era of alchemy was in the process of being replaced by philosophical chemistry.

Christianity
see **Early Christianity**

Church furnishings
see **Post-Reformation church furnishing; Pre-Reformation church furnishings and relics**

Clarsachs
see **Harps**

Clocks
see also **Horology**

The National Museums have important horological collections tracing the evolution of clock-making and clock owning in Scotland from the early 17th century up to the 20th.

Mechanical timekeeping probably developed with the expansion of the burghs, where merchants and craftsmen required a more reliable method of telling the time than by observing the sun. In the late medieval period, therefore, many burghs acquired a common clock, or 'toun knock'. The first recorded mention of a clock in Scotland concerns the town clock of Aberdeen.

The craftsmen who built or maintained these clocks, however, were originally members of the locksmith's trade. Clock-making as a separate craft did not appear in Scotland until September 1647, when the sons of one James Smith were the first men to be admitted to the Incorporation of Hammermen of Edinburgh as 'knocksmiths' in their own right. This suggests that clockmakers had become numerous and important enough to form a separate trade.

One of the Museums' earliest surviving watches by a Scottish maker shows that the craft had reached a fairly advanced stage by about 1600. This is by David Ramsay, watch-maker to James VI, and was supposedly given by the King to one of his favourites, Robert Carr, 1st Earl of Somerset, whose arms are engraved on it. Ramsay was one of the craftsmen who followed James to London in 1603, where he became one of the founder members of the Clock-maker's Company.

courses. At these lectures it was reported that 'the ladies declare that there never was anything so delightful as these chemical flirtations'. Hope's excellent and extensive apparatus includes two items of particular interest: counter-current condensers in which a flow of water in an outer tube condenses vapour in a concentric inner one. These are now called Liebig condensers but they certainly predate the great German chemist Justus von Liebig after whom they are named. One, an attractive instrument with a decorated japanned tinned iron trough, may well be the earliest object of its kind to survive. Liebig condensers were vital for the development of organic chemistry where low-boiling-point liquids must be purified by distillation.

Perhaps the most evocative item in the Playfair Collection is a clumsy balance with a label stating that Black used it in his seminal experiments to characterize the properties of carbon dioxide, the first gas to be chemically identified. It is claimed that the experiments were also the first truly quantitative ones to be described. Black's

Gold and bronze artefacts, 800–500 BC, showing the importance of a warrior aristocracy in the later bronze age. **Bronze age goldwork; Bronze age sheet metalwork**

Throughout the 17th century the development of the craft accelerated, with an increased demand for domestic timepieces. By the middle of the century brass lantern clocks were popular. Lantern-like in shape, they usually stood on wall brackets and were weight driven, having a single bell and normally only one hand. There is a fine example by an Edinburgh craftsman, Humphrey Milne, in the collections.

The late 17th century saw the development of what was to become the most popular type of clock in Scotland: the longcase or grandfather clock. The most famous late 17th-century clock-maker whose work has survived was Paul Roumieu. His father, also Paul, arrived in Scotland from France sometime before 1677. A beautiful and elegant marquetry longcase clock in the Museums shows his skill at its best.

By the second half of the 18th century many Scottish clock-makers were producing a wide range of accurate astronomical clocks, musical clocks and 'performing' clocks with complicated automata. The final phase in the development of the longcase clock began with 'painted' dial clocks, which were popular from about 1790 to 1880. They were made, or assembled, in their thousands in virtually every town and large village in Scotland.

Their distinctive feature was a highly decorative painted face. Almost any popular image could be used in the arch of the dial, with scenes from Sir Walter Scott's novels being especially favoured. The corners were painted with illustrations which fell into convenient groups of four; extravagantly dressed ladies representing the four seasons were particularly common. Occasionally the scenes were more localized, as in the east-coast herring fleets which decorate the face of a clock by the Pittenweem maker, George Lumsden, now in the collections.

Coal, Oil and the Metals
see also Hydrocarbons

Because of the huge scale of the equipment used in the coal, oil and metal industries, models of such equipment

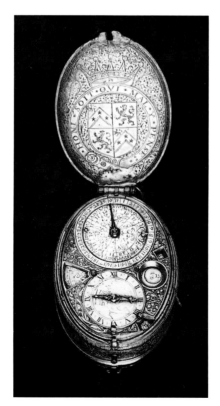

Watch by David Ramsay, about 1615, engraved with the arms of Robert Carr, 1st Earl of Somerset: thought to be a gift from James VI.

Brass lantern clock by Humphrey Milne, Edinburgh, about 1670.

Charles I commemorative jewellery.
Commemorative jewellery

'Stirling head', about 1540: carved wood medallion, allegedly representing James V, from a ceiling in the palace, Stirling Castle. **Carved and painted woodwork**

Longcase clock with marquetry case, by Paul Roumieu, Edinburgh, about 1700. **Clocks**

Set of chamber pipes from north-east Scotland, about 1815, and manuscript book of music which belonged to the owner of the pipes at that time. **Bagpipes**

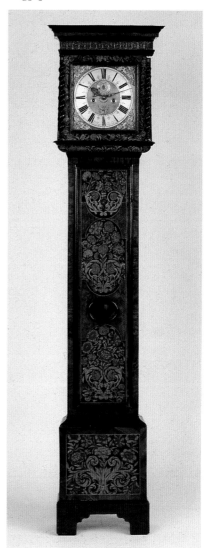

Union Bank of Scotland banknote for £1, 1921. **Banknotes**

Part of the early 17th-century painted ceiling from Dean House, near Edinburgh, showing a representation of the Sense of Hearing. **Carved and painted woodwork**

COAL OIL AND THE METALS

form a large and important part of the national collection. There is also a large number of hand tools and product samples.

Coal mining has a long history in Scotland and the collection includes a number of early wooden implements found at various times in old workings. There are many 19th- and 20th-century tools and items of equipment, some of which were purchased new for the Museums. The collection of miners' lamps is particularly noteworthy. Of the models, the most important is William Baird's Gartsherrie coal cutter of 1864. Driven by compressed air, this was the first coal cutter to be used on a significant scale.

The West Lothian shale oil industry, started in the 19th century by James 'Paraffin' Young, is represented by a series of models of the extraction and refining plant, together with samples of the various products.

Of the metal industries, iron and steel are by far the most important although some non-ferrous metals, particularly lead, were produced in Scotland. Important models made in the Museums include an early Bessemer steel-making plant and a particularly fine model of a late 19th-century blast furnace installed at Glengarnock in Ayrshire.

Fortunately at the time of the recent contraction in the Scottish steel industry it was possible for the Museums to acquire a small number of larger items of equipment. These include a rolling mill and its electric driving motor from the Victoria Works, Coatbridge. The mill was built in the 1920s by Murray & Paterson, also of Coatbridge. A large, 20-ton capacity, steam crane by Marshall Fleming &

Collection of miners' lamps, mid-19th to mid-20th century.

Jack of Motherwell and a scrap-shearing machine by the Airdrie Iron Company were acquired from the Lanarkshire Steelworks, Motherwell.

Coins

see also Banknotes; Trade tokens

The National Museums have an outstanding collection of several thousand Scottish coins representing almost all known types and varieties. There are also substantial holdings of English and foreign, including Roman, coins, largely through the discovery of coin hoards. In addition, there is a collection of 17th-century equipment from the Edinburgh mint.

Before the 12th century there is little evidence of a money economy and coins were not common. David I (1124–53) was the first Scottish king to mint coins, silver pennies with his bust on one side and a cross design on the other. Until the 1280s halfpennies and farthings were produced by halving and quartering pennies. Smaller coins then made a hesitant appearance, and in the 1350s larger coins, groats, each worth fourpence. The first gold coins, nobles, 6s 8d (33p), were also issued by David II at this time. They were not successful, but gold coins were reintroduced by Robert III (1390–1406) and became a regular part of the coinage from then on.

In the 15th century there was an increasing variety in coin types and designs, many of them distinctively Scottish. St Andrew first appeared on the gold lions of Robert III, unicorns on the coins of that name issued by James III (1460–88), and thistles on some of his groats. Many of the designs were very good, such as the James III groats issued from about 1485, with the first real coin portrait to be seen north of the Alps.

On the other hand the poverty of the country was reflected in the increasing debasement of the silver coinage until in some types there was so little silver that it was distinguished as an alloy, called billon. The first copper coinages were issued in the 1470s, but were so little liked that over 130 years passed before copper coins made a reappearance in the reign of James VI (1567–1625), this time for good.

During the 17th century the designs of silver and gold issues of Scotland and England were made more alike. The small change of the period, copper turners or bodles (twopences) and bawbees (sixpences) were uniquely Scottish. With the Union of the Parliaments in 1707 the Scottish coinage came to an end, to be replaced by a new British coinage based on the English standard and value.

Medieval coins were minted in several Scottish burghs, but from the reign of James IV (1488–1513) almost all Scottish coins were minted in Edinburgh.

Commemorative jewellery

Commemorative jewellery can be defined as articles worn in remembrance of an occasion, for example a political event, a defeat, or a royal event such as a coronation or a death. Generally the item bears an appropriate engraved or enamelled reference to the occasion. Rings are the most common form of commemorative jewellery although there are also examples of lockets, slides and brooches.

The first appearance of commemorative jewellery in any quantity was in the 17th century and was linked to the execution of Charles I. Much of the memorial jewellery dating from Charles's death (1649) is beautifully enamelled in black and white, while the bezels of many of the rings contain miniature portraits of the King or the initials C R worked in gold wire. A large collection of rings, brooches and slides (worn over a ribbon at the neck or wrist) are contained in the Museums' Rossignol Collection.

The deposing of James VII (1688) does not appear to have resulted in any extensive production of commemorative pieces. Indeed most Jacobite jewellery dates from the

Groat showing a portrait of James III,
about 1485.

period when the cause was effectively lost. A variety of rings were produced with images or symbols linked to Prince Charles Edward Stuart and his brother, Cardinal York, and the Seton Ring held in the Museums is a fine example. The hoop of the ring is made of four scrolls with the inscription 'C.P.R./DUM/SPIRAT/SPERO', (While I live I hope), and the bezel contains a miniature bust of Prince Charles Edward. The silver 'Disruption' brooches of 1843, an example of which is in the collection, were commercially made and sold as souvenirs, celebrating the formation of the Free Church in Scotland.

The items of jewellery so far described have all had associations with events of nationwide significance. Items were also made to mark events of a more localized or intimate nature. Mourning jewellery designed to hold a lock of hair of a deceased relative or friend became popular in the second half of the 18th century and by the 1840s some jewellery was made entirely of hair. Young ladies, indeed, were urged to learn the art of hair jewellery both as a social grace, and to guard against unscrupulous tradesmen who might substitute the hair of a stranger for that of a departed friend. Armed with a pair of tweezers, a knife, curling irons, gum and a porcelain palette, a Victorian lady could weave hair into a basket pattern or create a scene with weeping willows. By the 1860s this form of com-

memorative jewellery had ceased to be fashionable but brooches with a small compartment at the back for a lock of hair continued to be popular until the end of the 19th century. The Museums have an interesting collection of 'hair' reflecting many of the developments both of style and taste which took place during the period of its popularity.

Costume
see also **Military uniform: Rural homes**

The National Museums of Scotland have the largest collection of costumes in Scotland, which ranks as one of the five major collections in Britain. It comprises the former Royal Scottish Museum's collection which includes European folk and fashionable dress, the Charles Stewart collection of mainly fashionable dress, kept at Shambellie House, New Abbey, and the collection of the former National Museum of Antiquities of Scotland which includes clothes worn by Scots in Scotland and clothes made in Scotland.

The costume collection documents changes in fashion and materials over three centuries, and is a fascinating reflection of lifestyles and social attitudes. The earliest piece is probably the so-called Viking hood; the most

Maker's sample book of hair and mourning jewellery, 19th century.

recent dates from the 1980s. Although the Museums' aim is to collect a range of Scottish material reflecting different lifestyles, the very fabric of the clothes ensures that some pieces survive more readily than others. Clothes from the poorest members of society do not survive because they are worn out. The really wealthy gave their clothes away to their valets and maids as perquisites of their office, after which they were sold down the line. Therefore the collections reflect the middling ranges of society.

The collections have both the young girl's first ball dress and her grandmother's best black silk. There is a lack of 19th-century men's clothes after about 1840 because they

ceased to be colourful and distinctive, and were probably passed on to those less fortunate. However, evening suits survive in good numbers.

There are also specialist categories such as court suits, robes of Orders of Chivalry, and a rare herald's tabard of 1707–14. There is a splendid Privy Councillor's suit worn by a Scottish nobleman at George IV's Coronation in 1821. The Museums have a Newhaven fishwife's working dress and her gala outfit, and an East Lothian bondager's (farm servant's) clothes.

Also of great interest are three or four outfits found on bodies buried in peat bogs, mostly dating from the late

An outfit in Scottish tweed designed by Bill Gibb, commissioned by the Museums in 1985.

Clothes found on the body of a man buried in a bog at Gunnister, Shetland, about 1700.

Type specimen of the Carboniferous (350 million years ago) 'sea lily' (crinoid) *Woodocrinus liddesdalensis* Wright, from Roxburghshire.

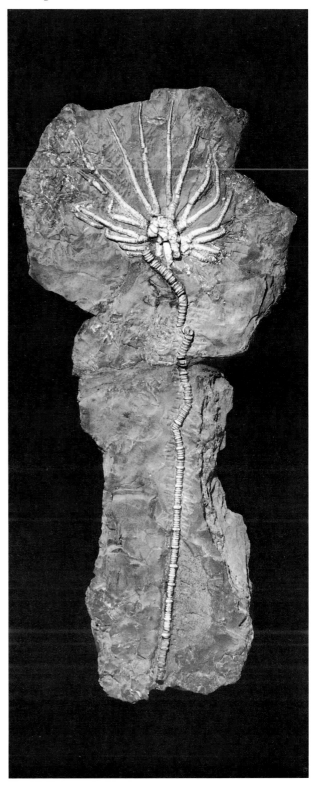

17th century. These, from remote areas of Scotland, show the clothes of less wealthy members of the community.

Amongst the fashionable dress there are garments from the leading Edinburgh and Glasgow stores, and from a high-class Aberdeen dressmaker, Helen Bagrie, as well as items bought from London and Paris fashion houses. There are labels from tailoring establishments, hatters, and shoemakers from all over Scotland and an impressive collection of babies' and children's wear, including Ayrshire robes and items from the 18th century.

Crinoids: fossil

Although they are called sea lilies from their flower-like shape, crinoids are marine animals related to sea urchins and starfish. Their five-armed bodies are usually supported on a stem anchored in the sea-floor by a root-like holdfast. The animal has an external skeleton of many lime carbonate plates, which after its death usually become separated. These plates are among the most common fossils (see **Fossils**) especially in limestones. Crinoids were known from fossils long before they were known as living animals: they have reduced in number and variety since their Palaeozoic heyday 530 to 260 million years ago (Ma). Most adult crinoids were then stalked but today are mainly stalkless and free-moving.

The National Museums have almost 5000 crinoids, of which nearly 1000 are cited in scientific papers. Most of these were bequeathed in 1958 by the amateur collector James Wright of Kirkcaldy, who published some forty papers on crinoids. His collection contains many fine specimens, mostly from the Carboniferous (360–290 Ma) of Fife. The Museums also have significant collections from the Ordovician (440 Ma) of Girvan and from the Silurian (430 Ma) of the Pentland Hills, collected by D Hardie and J Henderson in the last century.

Domestic metalwork
see also **Architectural metalwork**

The National Museums have a vast range of domestic items made of iron and copper alloys. A particular strength is the collection of medieval bronze vessels.

In the Middle Ages many essential domestic items were cast in bronze, particularly large three-legged cauldrons, ewers for pouring water to wash the hands, and candlesticks. Prior to the 14th century candlesticks were invariably of the pricket variety with a spike to hold the candle rather than a socket. It was only in the 18th century that bronze cooking pots were being replaced by pots cast in iron, many made by Scottish foundries. Some of the ewers are finely cast with dragonesque spouts, or are even in the form of animals, such as a lion-shaped example from Kilbirnie in Ayrshire. Although some of these bronze pots and ewers were being made in Scotland the majority were imported from the Continent. This was probably also the case with other items, such as spoons and knives.

Many pieces of household equipment and utensils were made of wrought iron, such as locks and keys, caskets and fireplace equipment.

Domestic silver

Objects of silver and gold have been made and used in Scotland since prehistoric times, and there are historical references to goldsmiths from at least the 13th century. It is not, however, until the mid-16th century that records allow us to identify individual makers with examples of their art.

By this date goldsmiths were established in the growing burghs of Scotland. In Edinburgh they had formed their own trade Incorporation by 1525, while elsewhere they belonged to the Incorporation of Hammermen. These organizations controlled all aspects of the working lives of their members, especially the right to admission, for no one could work in a burgh unless he was a member, or 'freeman': the medieval 'closed shop'! They also controlled the quality of members' work, something which was particularly important to the goldsmiths' trade as it was so obviously open to fraud (gold and silver, being too soft to be used in their natural state, have to be mixed or alloyed with other, cheaper metals to make them harder and more durable).

Many laws were passed to control fraud, and from an early date goldsmiths were obliged to stamp their wares with their personal mark and to have the quality of the metal tested by an official who would also stamp his mark and the mark of the town where it was made. These were the original 'hallmarks', one of the earliest forms of

Bronze aquamanile (ewer), 14th century, found in Kilbirnie Loch, Ayrshire.

consumer protection. They incidentally help historians to identify the makers and dates of early silver.

The National Museums' collections cover as wide a stylistic, chronological and geographical range as possible, building up a picture of the role of silver and silversmiths in Scottish history.

One of the earliest and most important pieces in the collection is the Galloway mazer, a maple-wood drinking bowl with silver-gilt rim and foot by James Gray of the Canongate. It is marked with the Canongate town mark of a stag. This, like most other town marks, was taken from the burgh's coat of arms. (Glasgow used the Tree, Fish and Bell, Inverness the Dromedary, Perth the Double-headed Eagle, etc.)

The only recorded Scottish mazer earlier than the mid-16th century is the unique Bute or Bannatyne mazer. Its central print dates from about 1320 and consists of a lion, representing King Robert Bruce, surrounded by six enamelled plaques bearing the arms of his captains. The maplewood bowl and unmarked silver mounts are later,

probably dating from the first half of the 16th century.

Edinburgh, whose mark was a three-towered castle, was Scotland's most important silver-producing centre because of its concentration of wealth and patronage. Its goldsmiths developed their own styles, characterized, in the early 18th century, by a well proportioned elegance. The ewer, basin and box made in 1706 by Thomas Ker for the 1st Earl of Hopetoun are outstanding examples of this. Edinburgh goldsmiths also produced more richly ornamented items, such as the magnificent travelling canteen of Prince Charles Edward Stuart, made in 1740–1 by the Jacobite Ebenezer Oliphant. Edinburgh goldsmiths kept to the forefront of the craft, reflecting current style and taste until the late 19th and early 20th century, when their numbers declined, probably due to competition from London, Birmingham or Sheffield.

Silversmiths in the other burghs of Scotland also grew in numbers and were producing fine wares. Glasgow, in particular, had many excellent craftsmen in the 18th and 19th centuries. Trade prospered there to such an extent

Claret jug by John Crichton, Edinburgh, 1883–4, engraved with the arms of the Incorporation of Goldsmiths of Edinburgh.

Thistle cup by Robert Bruce, Edinburgh, 1697–8.

that in 1819 an Assay Office was opened to cater for the city and the surrounding area.

Craftsmen in the smaller centres such as Tain, Dingwall and Elgin, tended to concentrate on more workaday items like spoons, forks and rings, probably reflecting the comparative wealth of their clients.

Since the Second World War there has been a revival of silversmithing and there are now a number of active small workshops. The Museums have been acquiring and commissioning new work, for example a silver and enamelled vase by Maureen Edgar, whose workshop is near Eyemouth, Berwickshire.

Early Christianity
see also **Pre-Reformation church furnishings and relics**

Christianity is now so much a part of our culture that it is perhaps necessary to remind ourselves that it was not adopted in Scotland until after the Romans abandoned Britain, and in many areas much later than that. The pattern and process of conversion can be glimpsed only from brief references in early historical documents. The archaeological evidence is not much more extensive and has its own levels of ambiguity.

The most widespread evidence consists in the large stone crosses and cross-slabs reflecting a range of influences from different areas. In the west, as at Iona, the crosses find parallels in contemporary Ireland whereas in the south, most spectacularly at Ruthwell, Dumfriesshire, the styles of Northumbria are evident. In the Pictish northeast, the cross-slabs appear as giant versions of manuscript pages complete with complex interlace decoration. They are all variants in a Christian milieu that had much in common. Both Northumbria and the Picts were converted from Iona with its strong Irish connections.

Most of this sculpture dates from centuries after AD 750 when Christianity already had a firm hold as the official religion of most of what we now call Scotland. From the conversion period little survives, the most important item being the Monymusk reliquary. This is one of only nine surviving Irish-Scottish house-shaped shrines now scattered as far afield as Italy and Norway. Essentially, these small reliquaries were designed for travel with individual missionaries and not for installation in a particular church. The reliquary is reputedly associated with St Columba and is elaborately decorated. Dating from around AD 750, its decoration is remarkable for the virtual absence of any obviously Christian iconography, suggesting perhaps that its

missionary potential was enhanced by symbols readily interpretable by pagans.

Other early Christian items such as the large bronze and iron bells traditionally assumed, on no very strong evidence, to be for religious purposes are difficult to date because of their simplicity. Several survive only because of their supposed associations with saints and their subsequent encasement in elaborate reliquaries. A similar fate befell St Fillan's crosier, apparently of late 11th-century date.

Finally, there are a few objects, not in their form religious but to which Christian inscriptions have been added. A fine example is the silver-gilt chape from the St Ninian's Isle Treasure (see **St Ninian's Isle Treasure**). Yet even here there are difficulties. The symbolism which it is suggested is to be found in the Hunterston brooch (see **Pseudo-penannular brooches**) warns against expecting

The crosier shrine, or *coicrich*, of St Fillan, 15th century, but incorporating earlier work.

all Christian images of this period to be immediately intelligible to the late 20th-century eye.

Edinburgh shawls
see **Textiles**

Electricity
see also **History of physical science; Public utilities**

Electricity was the new science of the 18th century. The invention of the Leiden Jar in 1745 enabled the charge from a frictional generator to be stored, built up and released on demand. Not only could the electrical phenomena *per se* be studied, but the effect of the electrical 'fluid' provided new areas of investigation. All the Scottish electrical machines in the collections are 19th century. There is a small globe machine by Lunan of Aberdeen, and a large disc machine by Kemp of Edinburgh. An unsigned cylinder machine, of late 18th-century design, is of particular interest as it came from the Royal Medical Society, and is a reminder that electrotherapy has a long history.

Following Volta's 1800 invention of what we would now call the battery, current electricity provided a fruitful area of study. There is an early voltaic pile from the Playfair Collection, and several experimental batteries designed and tested by the Edinburgh chemical instrument-maker K T Kemp in the late 1820s. The development of the electric telegraph and the electric dynamo spawned whole new industries. Vital instrumentation was provided by William Thomson's precise electrical measuring devices, made by White of Glasgow in the second half of the 19th century. The collections contain a representative selection, including reflecting galvanometers and current meters.

Embroidery

The National Museums' collection of embroidery includes pieces from nearly every European country, much of it on folk costumes. From Britain the range is comprehensive, starting with early 14th-century *opus Anglicanum* and ending with work from the present day. *Opus Anglicanum* is the work created in professional embroidery workshops, mainly in London; ecclesiastical vestments show some surviving examples.

Firmly provenanced Scottish pieces before the 18th century are rare but those that are known are interesting and important. They include the Fetternear Banner, probably the only surviving pre-Reformation religious

embroidery. Secular pieces include the wall hangings known as the Loch Leven and Linlithgow hangings. These were made by professional embroiderers probably in the early 17th century, although they have been erroneously ascribed to Mary, Queen of Scots.

Domestic needlework of the 17th century is a particular strongpoint of the collection although most of the work is by unknown women. However, the Lady Campbell of Glenorchy proudly signed and dated a set of bed valances of 1632.

The Museums' collection of samplers comprises a charming group of embroideries, with about a hundred named and dated examples from 1712 to 1939. The Scottish embroideress tended to include all the family's initials and use a specific range of motifs more frequently than her English and Welsh counterparts.

Although little is known about the professional em-

Betty Plenderleath's sampler, made in 1745 at Mrs Seton's school, Edinburgh.

Herald's tabard, satin embroidered in coloured and metal thread, featuring the coat of arms as borne in Scotland 1707–14.

broidery workshops that must have existed before the 19th century, the collections include some items which would have been made in them, such as the herald's tabards. From the 19th century there are examples of Ayrshire embroidery including a rare sampler of designs of about 1800 done in tambour work, the forerunner of the more usual satin-stitch embroidery with needlelace fillings.

The 20th-century collection includes work by Jessie Newbery and Anne Macbeth of the Glasgow School of Art, Louisa Chart of Edinburgh and Dorothy Angus of Aberdeen. This part of the collection was greatly strengthened by gifts following the breakup in 1961 of the Needlework Development Scheme, a Scottish-based scheme whose aim had been to bring good embroidery design into schools.

Engineering
see also Lighthouses; Power for industry; Ships and marine engineering

The production of machine tools ('machines which make machines') was significant in Scotland. Among the tools in the collection are a set of plate-bending rolls by Craig & Donald and a plate-edge planing machine by Thomas

Shanks, both of Johnstone. These machines were used in such places as boiler-making shops. Another Johnstone firm, John Lang, represented in the collection by a brass-finisher's lathe of the 1890s, is particularly noteworthy because at an early date the firm began to specialize almost entirely in lathes and became one of the largest makers of these tools. Langs were for many years unique in specializing to this degree. Tool-making was not confined to the west of Scotland; there is a steam hammer, probably dating from the last quarter of the 19th century, made by Davis & Primrose of Leith.

Hydraulic machinery was another important branch of the industry, represented in the collection by a hydraulic pump which formed part of the operating mechanism for a swing bridge. This dates from the early years of the 20th century and was a product of the Kilmarnock works of Glenfield & Kennedy. Another important item is a hydraulic riveting machine used in structural engineering work, made by Sir William Arrol, Glasgow.

A number of Scottish engineering firms made certain products, such as sugar processing machinery, for which the market was entirely overseas. While a certain amount of sugar refining was carried on in Britain, all the cane crushing was done overseas where the cane was grown.

Water scorpion (eurypterid) *Paracarcinosoma* from the Silurian (430 million years ago) of Lesmahagow, Lanarkshire.

However, the Museums have a model of a sugar-cane mill, by A F Craig of Paisley, one of half a dozen or more Scottish firms who were at one time engaged in this branch of engineering.

Eurypterids

Eurypterids are extinct water-scorpions which lived in Ordovician to Permian times, 480 to 260 million years ago (Ma). They are closely related to horseshoe crabs, and to arachnids such as spiders and scorpions, in having a pair of jointed claws on the first of their six head limbs. In living arachnids these claws are minute, but in some eurypterids they were gigantic, over $6\frac{1}{2}$ in (17 cm) long. Eurypterids range in size from small forms averaging less than 6 in (15 cm) long, up to some of the largest arthropods known. At over $2\frac{1}{2}$ yd (2.5 m) long with claws extended, they must have been powerful predators.

There are more than 800 specimens in the national collections, about 180 being important as type specimens (see **Fossils**). Many of these were described in an 1859 monograph by T H Huxley and J W Salter, one of the earliest significant accounts of eurypterids.

Eurypterids are relatively abundant and diverse in shallow water deposits of various ages in Scotland. Silurian (430 Ma) faunas are found at Lesmahagow, Lanarkshire and in the Pentland Hills. Although of similar age these faunas differ. Those of the Pentlands are dominated by long-legged forms adapted for walking over shallow sea floors, whilst more of the Lesmahagow forms were swimmers. One of the Old Red Sandstone (400 Ma) eurypterids of Angus approached two metres in length. Its ornament suggested feathers to the quarrymen, who called these eurypterids 'Seraphim'. This scale-like ornament misled Agassiz (see **Fishes**) into thinking they were fishes, and it was some years before their true nature was recognized.

Another eurypterid from Angus, one of many in the James Powrie Collection, reveals details of the paired gills on the underside of these animals. Although most evidence suggests eurypterids were aquatic for most of their lives, recent interpretation of such gills suggests some eurypterids may have been amphibious. Carboniferous (360–300 Ma) eurypterids are rarer, frequently fragmentary and hence poorly known. Some of the first eurypterids described, as well as some being currently collected, come from the Bathgate Carboniferous (340 Ma) (see **Amphibians: fossil**). These include large forms up to two metres long with combs on their limbs, possibly for filter feeding.

Farming and fishing

see also **Man and beast; Rural homes; Rural skills and trades**

It goes without saying that farming is fundamental to the way we live. This is as true today when about three per cent of the population work on the land as two centuries ago when farming occupied most people. The interval has seen the industrialization of agriculture, producing an ample and reliable source of food that would have astonished our forebears. Recording the material culture of this historically important change is thus a vital concern of the National Museums. The objects fall into three broad sections: hand tools, ox- or horse-worked items, and those associated with powered mechanization.

The hand tools and hand-worked machinery cover the range of crop husbandry and grain processing, from spades, the Highland *cas chrom* and Shetland *delling* spade, hand harrows, *heuks*, scythes, to the flails and *wechts* for thrashing and winnowing, and many less obvious but vital objects, from sowing sheets and hand turnip seeders to *thrawcruiks* for making straw ropes. The detail of these tools is particularly interesting because it often reveals both regional patterns and the structure of pre-industrial technology. There is small-scale barn machinery, such as the large collection of winnowing machines which shows the development of Andrew Meikle's invention both as made by local joiners and serially produced by manufacturers.

The horse-worked implements include ploughs and the wide variety of field machinery developed during the 19th century. Some of the important iron parts from the cattle-worked old Scotch plough survive, as do some of the now irreplaceable examples of single-stilted ploughs from the Northern and Western Isles. Most of the comprehensive plough collection demonstrates the development from the James Small-type improved swing plough to mass-produced ploughs of the 19th and 20th centuries. Such a basic function as cultivation has produced many special ploughs, from the graceful smiddy-made, long-boarded competition ploughs to reversible, drill, drainage and potato-lifting ploughs, all of which are well represented in the collection.

Although it was prominent for only 100 years, the horse-worked machinery of the 19th century was a vital development stage in the industrialization of agriculture. Harvesting machinery is well represented, showing the technical development of the reaper and binder up to semi-mounted tractor models. This part of the collection is a good record of light engineering as well as farming, illustrating the importance of small-town manufacturing to the rural economy of 19th- and early 20th-century Scotland.

Much of the earlier era of improved horse-worked implements is drawn together by the Highland and Agricultural Society of Scotland Collection. The Society began collecting in the late 18th century and the particular value of the material is that it reveals the experimental stages behind new developments. It includes, for instance, the first reaping machines that nearly worked, as well as Patrick Bell's reaper of 1828, the first that *did* work.

The coming of powered mechanization and bulk handling, and with that the demise of horse-working in the 1950s and 60s, virtually completed the industrialization of agriculture. The collection charts this in some detail, with examples of steam engines used to drive both barn threshing mills and travelling mills, and gas engines. Early tractors and trailing ploughs, such as the first reaping machines illustrate early development. The early combine harvesters made before the 'take-off' post-war stage, and the early Ferguson-system tractors and mounted implements were not only a great novelty in their day, but also represent the fruition of an era of change of great historical importance.

Related to the farmers' tools are those of fishermen, and they are of particular importance where fishing and farming were complementary as in the crofting counties of Scotland. The collection includes a range of gear from those areas, of the kind used from small open boats – great and *smaa* lines, and the creels, skulls, baiting boards and equipment that went with them – as well as the rippers, hand lines and poke-nets used for inshore and rock fishing.

Fishes: fossil

The term 'fish' generally includes all backboned animals which have lived in water throughout their history. This is an amazingly diverse group, even if they all look alike to us. For example, animals with bony or cartilaginous skeletons, with many gill openings or just one pair, and even with or without jaws, are all called fish. They originated more than 500 million years ago (Ma), but were very rare until the late Silurian (about 425 Ma).

Thereafter they flourished, and the Devonian period (about 410–360 Ma, when Old Red Sandstone rocks were laid down in Scotland) is known as the 'Age of Fishes'; although still very primitive, they were then the highest

Bondagers dressing potatoes at West
Pilton, Midlothian, 1912. *(James Watt;
SEA)*

A pair of horse in show harness at a
ploughing match in Perthshire, probably
1930s. *(Henry Davidson, Bankfoot; SEA)*

forms of backboned animal. During this time they gave rise to amphibians (see **Amphibians: fossil**) which began living on land.

The majority of these strange, early armoured fishes became extinct at the end of that period, and were replaced by the somewhat more normal-looking sharks, lungfish, lobe-fins and ray-fins of the Carboniferous (about 360–290 Ma). They were replaced in turn by structurally more and more advanced fishes, culminating in today's extremely successful ray-fins and sharks.

Much of Lowland and eastern Scotland (with scattered localities elsewhere) is formed from Devonian and Carboniferous rocks rich in fossils from this crucial early phase of fish history, and the National Museums have one of the finest collections in the world. Nineteenth-century discoveries of Scottish fishes, from the Old Red Sandstone in particular, were linked with important episodes in the history of geological science, enhancing their interest and value. Fossil fishes were brought to the attention of scientists in the late 1820s, and Robert Jameson, professor of natural history at Edinburgh University, at once began collecting specimens from Caithness and Banffshire for the College Museum (later inherited by the National Museums).

A Swiss professor, Louis Agassiz, made it his ambition to name and describe all known fossil fishes, and visited Scotland in 1834 to study them. This stimulated a burst of discoveries which were illustrated for his great work *Recherches sur les Poissons Fossiles* (1833–43). He is now famous as the founder of the scientific study of fossil fishes, and the National Museums house many of his type specimens (see **Fossils**).

Fossil fishes were also discovered at Cromarty in the early 1830s by the stonemason, Hugh Miller, later a famous writer. He found several forms recognizable as fish, but there were others so strange as to defy comprehension, and he did not know anyone able to help him. He wrote about them, however, in a book about Cromarty published in 1835. This was noticed by a geologist who put him in touch with Agassiz and others. Such contacts gave Miller the knowledge and confidence to describe his own fossils, using Agassiz's names. The strangest of all was *Pterichthyodes milleri* (Miller's winged fish), earlier confused with other armoured fishes and variously identified by Murchison, Lyell and others as tortoises, crustaceans, rays or beetles! After his death in 1856, Hugh Miller's extensive and important material was acquired for the national collections by public subscription.

From 1875 to 1914 the collections were in the care of the eminent palaeontologist, Dr R H Traquair, who studied

Title page from *Poissons Fossiles du Vieux Grès Rouge* (Fossil Fishes of the Old Red Sandstone), Scottish supplement to *Recherches sur les Poissons Fossiles* by Louis Agassiz, 1844–5.

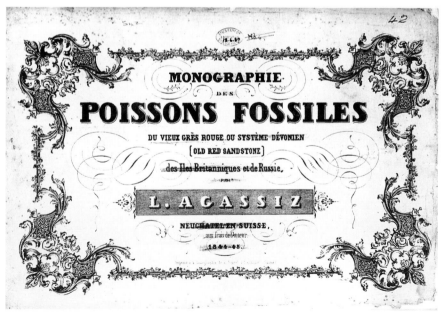

and described many new forms, made a notable collection himself and acquired numerous large collections. Those of James Powrie of Reswallie, Angus, and Charles Peach (Old Red Sandstone), James Neilson (Carboniferous), the Royal Society of Edinburgh and the Highland and Agricultural Society (general museum collections) are particularly important. Now that quarries and mines are no longer worked by hand, and many have closed, such riches are irreplaceable.

Since that time the Museums' collections have continued to grow steadily, and now number more than 20,000 specimens. Recent significant additions have been Stan Wood's new material from the Lothians, and the historic collection of Lady Gordon Cumming of Altyre, Morayshire, made in the 1840s. The collections incorporate important faunas, for example those from Lesmahagow, Lanarkshire (Silurian); Turin Hill, Angus; Lethen Bar, Nairnshire; Dura Den, Fife (Devonian); Eskdale, Dumfriesshire, and Wardie, Edinburgh (Carboniferous) which provide windows on fish life and evolution in the past.

Fishing gear
see **Farming and fishing**

Flags
see also **Embroidery; Pre-Reformation church furnishings and relics**

Flags have always had special importance to the armed services, whether as symbols of national or regimental identity or as means of communication. Ever since armies or fleets first went into battle they have needed clear signs giving details of units' locations. The use of such symbols spread to camps and barracks. The first thing a regiment would do on entering its billet for the night would be to display its flag or colour in a prominent place to give notice of its presence. The colour also served as a rallying point in battle. The ceremony of trooping the colour, now an enshrined part of the British Army's tradition, has its origins in the regimental colour being marched through the ranks to make all concerned familiar with it.

In infantry regiments the colours (two per battalion) developed a spiritual importance in addition to their practical function. To this day they are regarded as symbolizing the heart of a regiment and as such are treated with great ceremony and respect. Much the same applies in cavalry regiments to their standards and guidons (small pennants). The principal colour in an infantry regiment is that of the king or queen. This is the union flag

Regimental pipe banner of The Royal Scots, about 1910.

A selection of Scottish glass, from the 18th, 19th and 20th centuries. **Glass**

embroidered with selected emblems and titles of battles in which the regiment played a prominent part (known as battle honours). The second colour is called the regimental colour and is of the facing colour of the regiment with the union flag in the canton, the square in the corner. The whole is decorated with selected emblems and battle honours.

At one time each company of a regiment had its own colour, a tradition still carried on in foot guards' regiments. In Scottish regiments something of this practice is continued in the use of pipe banners. These are tied to the largest drone of a set of pipes and bear badges and titles similar to those employed on a colour. An officer in command of a company is permitted to have his personal arms displayed on one of the regiment's pipe banners. The Scottish United Services Museum contains a wide range of examples of regimental colours and pipe banners.

When colours were carried into battle there was always the risk of them being captured by the enemy. This was regarded as a great disgrace to the regiment. Conversely, if a regiment captured the colour of an enemy, this afforded great prestige. The taking of the Eagle and Standard of the French 45th Regiment at Waterloo by a sergeant of the Royal Scots Greys was regarded as so significant that the regiment's badge was changed to a French eagle. Both the gilt-metal eagle and standard are in the collection of the Scottish United Services Museum. Also in the Museum are the earliest surviving pair of British regimental colours, those of Barrell's Regiment, carried at Culloden in 1746.

Fossils
see also **Amphibians: fossil; Crinoids: fossil; Eurypterids; Fishes: fossil; Plants: fossil Reptiles: fossil**

Fossils are traces of ancient life. They are not only the actual remains of organisms, eg shells, but also the results of their activity, eg burrows and footprints (see **Reptiles: fossil**). Fossils are vital to geologists: they permit rocks of the same age to be recognized and correlated with one another; they often indicate the nature of the environment in which rocks formed, and they document the course of evolution.

The collection exceeds 100,000 specimens. Many of these come from Scotland and some are of historic importance, such as those forming the basis of John Fleming's *History of British Animals* (1828). Many of these specimens were collected by largely self-taught, 19th-century pioneers, the most famous of whom was Hugh Miller, stonemason and writer. The Museums have a policy of

A selection of John Fleming's collection of Carboniferous (350 million years ago) fossils, many of which were first named in his *History of British Animals* 1828, or in the later publications shown here.

The Galloway mazer by James Gray, Canongate, 1569. **Domestic silver**

Oil painting of a meal break in the harvest field at Auchendinny, Midlothian, early to mid-19th century. **Farming and fishing**

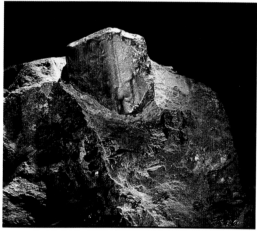

Red mahogany fly table by Andrew
Fleming of Kirkcaldy, about 1830.
Furniture

Sapphire crystal in volcanic rock from
Loch Roag, Isle of Lewis. **Gems**

One of a set of three embroidered panels
by Phoebe Traquair, 1904, showing a
scene from Spenser's *Faerie Queene*.
Embroidery

Slab of Upper Old Red Sandstone (about 360 million years ago) from Dura Den, Fife, a fossil 'graveyard', containing several different species of fish: the large fish is 100 mm across. **Fishes: fossil**

Colours of Barrell's Regiment of Foot (now part of the King's Own Royal Border Regiment) carried at Culloden, 1746. **Flags**

building on existing strengths in the collections. These are internationally important as they contain many type specimens: those which were named as new species or which, by being illustrated and described in publications, are the basis of knowledge of those particular animals and plants. Such original descriptions of extinct organisms are being constantly revised, and the original specimens reappraised by research workers in the light of new discoveries.

Scotland is rich in fossils of the Palaeozoic, 600 to 250 million years ago (Ma). Many of these are unusual forms that evolved in practically unique shallow water situations. Some are exceptionally well-preserved soft-bodied organisms such as the animal that bore the long-known but enigmatic teeth called conodonts. This was first found complete only in 1982 in the Edinburgh Carboniferous (340 Ma).

Among the many important collections of invertebrates (animals without backbones) are those of Professor H A Nicholson, from the Girvan Ordovician (450 Ma). He was one of the first to use thin sections, about 1000 of which are in the National Museums, to study corals and bryozoans. Silurian (430 Ma) fossils include those from Lesmahagow, Lanarkshire (see **Eurypterids**) and especially the Pentlands.

The collections are particularly rich in Carboniferous fossils, many from the Glasgow region. Robert Dunlop's collection, which includes that of quarrymaster Robert Craig, numbers over 20,000 specimens. Jurassic (155 Ma) fossils include ammonites collected by Hugh Miller, some of which have only recently been described as new species. Such discoveries continue to be made in the existing collections but emphasis has shifted from description towards studying the ecology and context of fossils, for which larger samples are required (see **Amphibians: fossil**).

Furniture

Furniture and fittings have always been important elements in the Museums' collections, although early examples (before the 17th century) are rare in Scotland both within and outwith the Museums. Amongst the earliest Scottish pieces are chairs with inscriptions and dates. This type of chair was generally made to commemorate a marriage, with the date, initials, and often a coat of arms. The Museums have a number of 'marriage' chairs, but perhaps the most notable example of a chair recording historical events is the Douglas Genealogical chair. The cresting rail and the back of the chair are carved with details of the

lineage of a branch of the Douglas family, the earliest decipherable date 1057. The chair, of oak, was made for Sir William Douglas of Glenbervie and his wife Anne and dates from 1665.

The early 18th century saw a new stimulus to the furniture trade with the publication of Thomas Chippendale's pattern book, *The Gentleman and Cabinet-Maker's Director*. This not only changed the course of furniture design in England but also had a profound influence on Scottish styles. After its publication wrights were frequently asked

Oak armchair showing the genealogy of the Douglases of Glenbervie, about 1665.

to make furniture according to 'English' designs. Cabinet-making took place in many parts of Scotland, though predominantly in Edinburgh.

In the early 19th century cabinet-making continued to expand throughout Scotland. James Mein of Kelso, for example, produced furniture for, amongst other patrons, the Earl of Haddington at Mellerstain in Roxburghshire. Mein also produced smaller items such as a mahogany wine slide and a lacebasket, about 1825. Both are in the Museums' collections. In the 1820s and 30s George Beath of Perth, James Creighton of Dumfries and Andrew Fleming of Kirkcaldy all produced well-made furniture, which is represented in the collections.

At this time there was also a gradual move away from the more traditional 'bespoke' furniture, and warerooms with large stocks of furniture began to appear throughout Scotland. Wareroom stock could be of a standard range, but could also provide for the more specialized market. A Polyterpic table in the collections is an example of furniture produced for a limited market. The table was made by John Buchanan of Greenock in 1817 and combines the functions of a compendium of games, a tea table and a viewing apparatus. This highly original piece of furniture was sold from Buchanan's general warehouse.

The effects of mechanization on the industry in the later 19th century saw the rapid expansion of a number of firms and brought a boom in mass production. There was also an increasing interest in 'design' furniture. Firms such as Wylie and Lochhead of Glasgow and Whytock and Reid of Edinburgh not only produced ranges for the 'popular' market but also became involved with many of the influential designers and architects of the day. Whytock and Reid produced furniture, represented in the collections, for many of Sir Robert Lorimer's commissions, and Wylie and Lochhead were closely associated with the 'Glasgow style'. Associated with the latter are E A Taylor and George Logan, examples of whose work are in the collections. The Museums also have a small but important collection of furniture and fittings by Charles Rennie Mackintosh.

After the First World War an identifiable 'Scottish' style of furniture generally disappeared, with the exception of isolated items such as Orkney chairs which continued to be produced. Large companies such as the Scottish Cooperative Wholesale Society and many smaller independent firms continued to produce for the Scottish market but the furniture was without any strong or distinct regional characteristics and was indistinguishable from furniture produced for the English market.

The collection of 20th-century material continues. A notable addition from the late 1920s is a cabinet by Thomas Tait, architect of St Andrews House and of the 1938 Empire Exhibition in Glasgow. More recent material includes two thrones, called 'Toni' and 'Cleo', made in 1986 by Geoffrey Bonar, who works in Glasgow.

Games
see **Sports and games**

Gas
see **Public utilities**

Gems

Only a few Scottish minerals such as quartz, topaz, garnet and sapphire have the qualities of beauty, rarity and durability to qualify as gems. There are 33 cut stones, almost all from the Heddle collection (see **Minerals**), in the national collections. Quartz, the most widespread gem mineral, occurs as several coloured varieties.

The most renowned is the dark brown material known as cairngorm or smoky quartz, the colour of which is caused by natural radioactivity. The name first appears in the literature of the 18th century when there was an active local industry digging crystals from the screes on the Cairngorm Mountains. It became very popular in the 19th century when it was used extensively in Highland dress, but crystals are now quite rare. The pale brown to yellow variety known as citrine is found mostly in Perthshire. Amethyst, the purple variety, normally occurs as small crystals but the Museums have a 42-carat (5 carats equals 1 gram) stone cut from a crystal found near Grantown-on-Spey. Colourless rock crystal is the commonest variety and a 300-carat stone from the Cairngorm Mountains is the largest Scottish quartz gem in the National Museums.

The Cairngorm Mountains and Beinn Bhreac in Sutherland are the major localities for topaz. Crystals which occur sparingly there were produced in the final stages of granite crystallization. Crystals tend to be pale blue and fine gems up to 37 carats have been cut.

Garnets, the second most common gem, are generally so fractured as to make them unsuitable as gems. Vibrant red garnets called pyrope found in volcanic rock at Elie Ness, Fife, and known as Elie rubies have been cut into small, 2-carat gems. Small polished fragments are also threaded into pieces of jewellery. Until recently sapphire had been found only as small plates, but now larger ($1\frac{3}{4}$ in 4.5 cm), fractured crystals have been found in volcanic rock on the Isle of Lewis. These are the largest sapphires in Britain and a flawless 2.9-carat stone has been cut from a fragment collected by Museums staff.

Several Scottish rivers, most notably the River Tay, contain freshwater mussels which occasionally produce pearls. These come in a range of colours, the most desirable being a plum-coloured blush of which the Museums have a representative selection.

Other gem-quality minerals that occasionally occur are beryl, apatite, prehite, tourmaline, fluorite and kyanite.

Glass

The history of glass in Scotland parallels the history of glass-making in Europe and the Middle East. Most of the information and surviving specimens come from outwith Scotland, but stray finds of material and stray references suggest that Scotland was certainly not devoid of glass or of a rudimentary glass industry even in the early medieval period. Excavations of Roman and Viking-period sites have yielded glass objects both decorative and functional, the exquisite blown glass vessel from the Roman camp at Newstead, Roxburghshire being an outstanding example.

Stained glass fragments in the National Museums from the great religious houses of Melrose, Dunfermline, Lindores, Cambuskenneth and Coldingham indicate that medieval Scotland imported coloured glass. The vigorous economic activities of some monasteries suggest that, with plentiful natural resources to hand such as silica in the form of sand, and alkali in the form of kelp or wood ash, glass was being made in Scotland at an early period. A reference to glass being made near Falkland in Fife about 1506 strengthens this theory.

Some of the most widely sought-after glass in medieval Europe came directly from Venice, or was later made in imitation of Venetian glass by German craftsmen. The *façon de Venise* techniques set the standard from the Renaissance for fine quality glass. An example is the Pitfirrane goblet associated with James VI.

While importing glass from England and the Continent, Scotland was also making glass both in sheet form for windows (known as 'braid glass') and in blown and blown-moulded form for drinking vessels and containers. Scotland shared in the quickening industrial pace of 16th-century Europe and encouraged her own glass-making industry. James VI granted a patent in favour of a glass factory at Wemyss in Fife in order to improve or to establish and protect glass-making.

The Pitfirrane goblet, a Venetian-style glass said to have been James VI's stirrup cup.

In the course of the 17th century, glassware production was established on both sides of the Forth. After about 1682 lead crystal was made in imitation of George Ravenscroft's significant experiments in London in fusing glass with oxide of lead. Fine examples of the 'rummer', a large bowled and short stemmed drinking glass, decorated with fluting and wheel-engraved pictorial scenes or commemorative portraits, are represented in the collections.

A vigorous tradition of conviviality and of fine wine

Jacobite wine glasses engraved with
anthem, portrait and symbols of the
exiled Stuart monarchy.

being enjoyed from fine glass ensured a growing demand
for glass products in 18th-century Scotland. This, together
with technical advances, made Britain one of the leading
centres of glass production in Europe. Wine glasses developed an artistry of their own, the most notable feature
of which was the decoration of the stems including air-
twist and opaque-coloured twist spirals. This particularly
distinctive type of table glass included wine glasses and
goblets engraved with Jacobite emblems and slogans
which were as much an English as a Scottish product,
and encouraged a covert support of the exiled Stuart
monarchy. The political tensions of the day kept much of
the evidence of Jacobite glass manufacture a secret.

With the Industrial Revolution in the late 18th century
investment in the heavy and extractive industries, for
example coal, meant that integrated ventures such as glass
manufacture benefited. Glassworks were established in
Edinburgh, Leith, Prestonpans, Perth, Dundee, Alloa,
Glasgow, Dumbarton and Greenock, and some of their
initial success lay in almost mass production for export,
especially to North America. In spite of a marked decline
in the industry in Scotland, glass-making enjoyed something of an artistic renaissance between the World Wars
with new ranges of decorative art glass. Monart glass was
produced in Perth from 1924 onward by Moncrieffs after
Salvador Ysart, a Spaniard who had worked at the
Bacovat factory in France, joined the firm. He and his sons
produced a range of glass products in a brightly coloured,
mottled glass. After 1946 some of the family set up on their
own in Perth producing Vasart glass in paler colours. The
collections contain examples of both.

Recent acquisitions include a special piece of engraved
glass, entitled 'Doors on the Past', commissioned from the
artist Alison Kinnaird to mark the formation of the
National Museums of Scotland on 1 October 1985.

Goldwork
see **Bronze age goldwork; Military art; Military
weapons; Viking goldwork**

Graves
see **Bronze age dagger graves**

Harps

The small harp or *clarsach* is familiar as the emblem of
Irish nationality, and yet some of the earliest evidence for
it belongs to mainland Britain. The 12th-century monk

and scholar, Gerald of Wales, praised the skill of harpers
in Scotland, Ireland and Wales and singled out the harpers
of Scotland for their excellence and inspiration which
drew musicians from the other Celtic communities to learn
from them.

The Highland harps in the National Museums, known
as the Queen Mary harp and the Lamont harp, are two of
the three oldest surviving, dating to the 15th or perhaps
early 16th century. The third, the celebrated Trinity College harp in Dublin, is strikingly similar to the Queen
Mary harp and may perhaps have been made by the same
craftsman. The Highlands and Islands of Scotland were
closely linked to Ireland by cultural and economic ties, at
least until the 17th century.

There are many examples in Scotland of harpers holding

The Lamont harp, early 16th century.

hereditary office in court and castle, fulfilling the ancient and fundamental function, together with the other ranks of the bardic orders, of composing and reciting praise song and poetry. The harper was a member of the professional and learned orders that survived longest in Gaelic society and there is considerable evidence in Gaelic of their function as composers of eulogy and elegy, of their teaching and apprenticeship which took them overseas to, for example, the 'schools in Ireland', of their travels between the great houses, and of their remuneration in goods and gear. The playing of the harp declined to extinction with the oppression of Gaelic society in the 18th century, to be revived in the late 19th when cultural characteristics of Celtic society were being espoused.

Heart brooches

Heart-shaped brooches have had a continuous history in Scotland for almost 300 years. The heart shape was known and used throughout Europe and beyond for centuries. In the medieval period it had a religious significance and was used in representations of the Arma Christi. The heart shape has a long history in heraldry, but it is as a symbol of love, betrothal and marriage that it appears most frequently in Scotland. Hearts are found on marriage lintels, carved chair backs, samplers and most particularly in the form of brooches.

Heart-shaped brooches were popular in 14th-century France, but no Scottish examples can safely be dated to much before 1700. The National Museums have a representative collection of over 300 examples, documenting the development of this attractive and particularly Scottish form of brooch.

The 18th-century brooches were usually of silver, although there are gold and base-metal examples and some set with paste stones and garnets. They have long been known as 'luckenbooth' brooches after the Luckenbooths, or small shops, which clustered round the High Kirk of St Giles in Edinburgh. As this was the goldsmiths' and jewellers' quarter, it is probable that the brooches were sold there, although the name itself cannot be traced before the late 19th century. 'Heart brooches' is therefore a more accurate term, although the brooches have also attracted other names, such as Queen Mary and witches' brooches.

Inscriptions on early examples prove that they were love tokens, probably given as engagement or marriage presents. 'My [heart] ye have, and thine I crave' is inscribed on one in the Museums. The placing of two hearts together also indicates love and the resultant M shape may explain the name Queen Mary brooch.

The brooches seem to have changed their function after marriage, and in the 18th century were worn as protection against witches. One given to the Museums in 1893 'was worn on the breast of the chemise by the grandmother of the donor, to prevent the witches from taking away her milk'. Children, boys as well girls, had heart brooches pinned under their petticoats 'for ... averting the evil eye and keeping away witches'. Keeping the charm hidden seems to have made it more powerful (see **Charms and amulets**).

Three silver heart brooches of the early 18th to early 19th century.

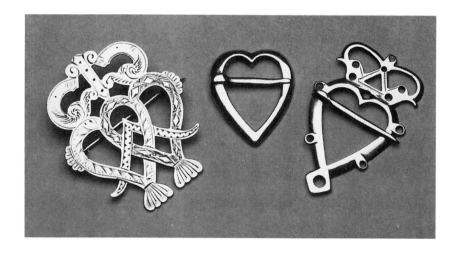

Towards the end of the 18th century the brooches became larger and more complicated. Most now had crowns above the hearts and twin hearts were common. Some were very fine pieces of jewellery, if lacking the naïve charm of the older forms, and were being made by established silversmiths in Edinburgh, Glasgow, Inverness and the north-east. They have continued in production right up to the present day and are particularly popular in tourist shops.

History of physical science
see also **Applied mathematics; Astronomy, navigation and surveying; Electricity; Horology; Meteorology; Oceanography; Optics; Sundials**

In 1662 Glasgow-born James Corss recorded with disarming honesty:

> I Have oftentimes lamented with myself to see so many Learned Mathematicians to arise in sundry parts of the world, and so few to appear in our Native Country. In other things we are parallel with (I shall not say in a superlative degree far above) other Nations; but in Arts and Sciences Mathematical, all exceed us. And had not that thrice Noble and Illustrious Lord, viz John Lord Nepper, Baron of Merchiston, &c. preserved the honour of our Nation by his admirable and more than mortal invention of Logarithms, we should have been buried in oblivion, in the memories of Forraign Nations.

John Napier's book *Mirifici logarithmorum canonis descriptio,* printed and published in Edinburgh in 1614, described a powerful and sophisticated mathematical invention, whose value was recognized by the scientific community of Europe. However, the invention of logarithms marked Scotland's first and for many decades sole significant contribution to the development of science.

Scottish material held under the umbrella of the History of Science Collections in the National Museums dates largely from the century following John Napier. Early material is somewhat sparse, and reflects the relative poverty of Scottish scientific achievement at the time. There is an astrolabe used by the cartographer Robert Gordon of Straloch (1580–1661), but it is an early 15th-century instrument of European origin. There is one of three known examples of the first logarithmic slide rule, made in Edinburgh in the mid-17th century, to the design published by the English mathematician William Oughtred in 1632. The maker was Robert Davenport, a London-trained instrument-maker, who in 1647 had been granted permission by the Town Council of Edinburgh to trade and undertake the 'teaching of his trade to such uthers as shall enter his service'.

During the 18th century the trade of scientific instrument-making became established in Edinburgh and Glasgow. At the time London was the premier European centre for the manufacture of instruments, so that Scottish craftsmen had to work against very strong competition. James Short (1710–68), orphaned son of an Edinburgh wright, specialized in the manufacture of reflecting telescopes. The high quality of his work was recognized by Colin MacLaurin, professor of mathematics in the University of Edinburgh. Encouraged by MacLaurin, Short

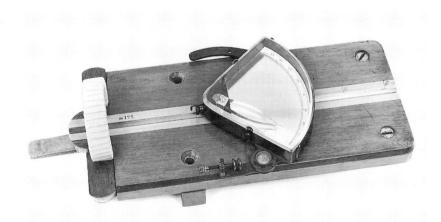

Graded current tangent galvanometer by James White, Glasgow, to the 1881 design of Sir William Thomson.

visited London, settling there permanently in 1738. He was elected a Fellow of the Royal Society of London, and served on its Council in his later years. For a living he made and sold reflecting telescopes to observatories and amateur astronomers across the world. There are examples of Short's Edinburgh- and London-made instruments in the collections.

Another instrument-maker to seek his fortune outside Scotland was James Watt who was initially a mathematical instrument-maker in Glasgow. The University employed him to clean and repair their instruments. Watt's attempts to put in order the scale model of a Newcomen engine belonging to the Natural Philosophy Class led to his radical improvement of the steam engine and the famous partnership with Matthew Boulton in Birmingham (see **Power for industry**). However, from 1757 to 1771 Watt ran a successful instrument-making business in Glasgow. There is a domestic barometer in the collection, the only known signed instrument made and sold by Watt.

James Watt's Glasgow business was continued by his senior journeyman John Gardner. The Gardner firm, despite many vicissitudes, continued to trade into the 20th century. Almost as long lived was an Edinburgh business established about the same time by John Miller, continued by his nephew, Alexander Adie, and his family until the late 19th century. Examples of the work of these dynasties of craftsmen, and of many other Scottish instrument-makers are to be found in the collections.

In the second half of the 19th century the Glasgow business begun by James White in 1850 established an international reputation. The key figure was not James White himself, but William Thomson (1824–1907), knighted 1866, created Lord Kelvin 1892, Professor of Natural Philosophy in the University of Glasgow, who became the major stakeholder in the business, and was responsible for the technical supremacy of its electrical instruments. Thomson made major theoretical contributions to a range of scientific topics and actively developed sensitive measuring devices. His interests in the new science of current electricity led to his appointment in 1857 as a director of the Atlantic Telegraph Company. The technical key to the success of the cable laid across the Atlantic in 1866 was immediately recognized as being Thomson's invention of a sensitive reflecting galvanometer, an instrument which permitted rapid and sustained transmission. The White business made Thomson's various patented telegraph instruments, and from the 1870s also made the improved marine compasses, designed as a result of Thomson's theoretical analysis and practical investigations

of the influence on the compass arising from the magnetism of the ship's hull. The National Museums have examples from the White factory of many of Thomson's instruments, providing a vivid illustration of his view that 'the life and soul of science is its practical application'.

Whilst instrument-making, like science, had some national characteristics, both have largely to be seen in a wider context. The case of the Thomson-designed instruments made by White of Glasgow is not typical, for generally most surviving Scottish-made artefacts relating to the practice and application of science in Scotland are no more than competent copies of tried and proved designs from London. In some cases there is a mechanically ingenious and sensible adaptation of a contemporary London design. In a few instances there is genuine originality and a standard of achievement as good as any in Europe.

The History of Science Collections of the National Museums contain examples falling into all these classes (see **Applied mathematics**; etc). In addition there are instruments made outwith Scotland which have an equally central position in the cultural history of the nation, for example the apparatus used for teaching in the Natural Philosophy Department of the University of Edinburgh.

There are many other items of individual significance and interest, each treasured for different reasons. Three 19th-century instruments will suffice as examples: an astronomical alt-azimuth instrument, used in navigation and surveying, made by Troughton of London and presented in 1806 to Professor John Playfair of the University of Edinburgh by students who had attended his classes in higher mathematics; an achromatic compound microscope made by Andrew Ross of London, with the inscription 'TO Dr John Hutton Balfour, Professor of Botany IN THE University of Glasgow BY THE LADIES Who attended his first Popular Course of Lectures DELIVERED IN 1843'; a three-axis theodolite developed by T Cooke and Sons of York about 1883, for Sir William Arrol, specifically for controlling the alignment of the cantilever arms and inclined members of that prime exemplar of late Victorian civil engineering, the Forth Bridge.

It would be a misunderstanding of the history of science to imagine that the instruments in the collections of the National Museums of Scotland are primarily relics related to important scientific discoveries. The very nature of scientific advance means that even where an observation or measurement stimulated a new way of understanding a natural phenomenon, or provided support for a new theoretical analysis, the original apparatus has rarely survived.

Experimental apparatus put together with the proverbial string and sealing wax is replaced by something purpose made, refined to extract greater potential from a new technique. Equipment used by one generation to make new discoveries is used to demonstrate and teach in the next, if its parts have not been cannibalized for other purposes. With a few exceptions, what survives in museum collections generally are instruments made to standard designs for routine work, the day-to-day tools of the scientific investigator, of the practitioner whose work is based on the application of scientific principles, and of the teacher demonstrating known phenomena.

From previous centuries there has survived another class of instruments: those related to science as a social activity. In Britain, from the 18th century until the latter part of the Victorian era, it was accepted that no man or woman could be considered truly educated unless he or she had at the very least some pretentions to the understanding of contemporary science. The public acceptance of science as a desirable, socially acceptable and praiseworthy intellectual activity was expressed in the use and ownership of scientific instruments. In some cases these instruments were no more than status symbols, in others

Mantel clock by Robert Bryson,
Edinburgh, 1804, with the rolling ball
escapement later patented by William
Congreve.

at best scientific toys, though such a judgement merely emphasizes the social status inherent in knowing about and understanding science.

An extreme example of such a development can be seen amongst microscopes in the 18th century. The collections of the National Museums include a number of small microscopes made in silver and dating from the mid-18th century. The designer and maker was an Edinburgh silversmith and optician, John Clark. These beautiful pieces of miniature engineering were sold to 'curious enquirers into the works of NATURE' complete with sets of ready mounted specimens to provide an interesting diversion. No serious scientific work could be done with instruments of this sort, but ownership was a positive expression of interest in seeing and marvelling at the hidden secrets of nature.

Hoards
see **Bronze age sheet metalwork; Iron age horse furniture; Iron age warfare; Jet necklaces; Stone axes; Traprain Treasure; Viking silver hoards**

Horology
see also **Clocks; History of physical science**

The National Museums' History of Science Collections have a special interest in precision horology. The most stringent demands for precision were associated with navigation (the chronometer) and astronomy (the astronomical regulator). It is in the latter area that the collections have considerable strength. An early and historically important clock is a 1756 regulator by John Shelton of London. The evidence suggests that it is the clock purchased by the Royal Society of London in 1760, and taken to St Helena to observe the 1761 Transit of Venus, to North America with Charles Mason and Jeremiah Dixon to measure the arc of the meridian (1765–7), to Tahiti with Captain James Cook to observe the 1769 Transit of Venus, and that it was subsequently used by Nevil Maskelyne on the 1774 expedition to Schiehallion in Perthshire to 'weigh the Earth'. After 1815 the history of the clock is firmly established – its travels included a spell at the Cape Observatory in South Africa (1829). From 1888 until 1904 it was used at the Ben Nevis Meteorological Observatory, ending its working life at the magnetic observatory at Eskdalemuir in Dumfriesshire.

There are electrical clocks made by Alexander Bain (1810–77), 'the father of electrical horology', who trained as a watchmaker in Wick, before working in Edinburgh and London.

There is a particular emphasis in the collections on high-precision electrical clocks. Regulators from the Royal Observatory, Edinburgh form the backbone of this part of the collections, with examples by Riefler of Munich (1909), Leroy of Paris (about 1920) and the prototype Shortt synchronome regulator of 1921 which set significant new standards for accuracy.

Horse furniture
see **Iron age horse furniture**

Hydrocarbons
see also **Coal, oil and the metals**

Hydrocarbons include oil, coal, bitumen and oil shales and have economic importance when found in quantity. The National Museums have a collection of nearly 200 hydrocarbons specimens, the majority in the Heddle Collection (see **Minerals**).

Coal, although worked since Roman times, was first mentioned in literature in 1291. The 'black stane' has had an immense impact on the social, economic and political development of the nation (see **Coal, oil and the metals**).

Torbanite, the oil-rich coal named after Torbane Hill near Bathgate, now worked out, was used by James 'Paraffin' Young in his pioneering process for the economic production of oil.

Oil shale, an important economic rock whose red waste bings transformed the landscape of the Midland Valley, yielded, ton for ton, only one third of the oil recovered from torbanite. It was exploited in response to the demand for oil and to circumvent Young's patent restrictions on coal-based oil extraction.

Fears of oil starvation during times of war prompted a programme of onshore drilling for oil. This has continued from 1918 until the present day and several very small fields have been found in the Midland Valley. Samples from these mainly historic fields, eg D'Arcy near Dalkeith and Dunnet mine near Broxburn, are in the collections. The major discoveries of oil were offshore in the North Sea, the first to be discovered in Scottish water being Montrose field, in 1969. The Museums hold a sample of North Sea oil, presented by BP.

Industry
see **Power for industry; Textile, paper and printing industries**

Instruments of punishment and torture

The post-Reformation Church in Scotland, through the Kirk Sessions, had a strong hold on the moral code of its congregations. The Museums have a varied collection of objects used by the Church to discipline and punish offenders against this code. Jougs, an iron collar attached to a wall by a chain, were generally used for minor offences, whereas members of the congregation who came before the Kirk Session for more serious misdemeanour, particularly adultery, were often punished by being made to sit on a stool of repentance during the service. The Museums have a fine example of a repentance stool from Old Greyfriars Church in Edinburgh and also a gown of repentance, made of sackcloth, from West Calder.

Judicial law in Scotland could exact more extreme punishments on wrongdoers and an Act of Parliament in 1574 required every town to have a prison with irons and stocks. Until its abolition in 1708, torture was a legally sanctioned part of criminal procedure in Scotland. By the 17th century, however, torture carried out under the auspices of the Privy Council was reserved for offenders whose crimes were seen as a threat to society – treason, witchcraft and religious non-conformity. The principal methods of torture in Scotland were the boots and the thumbscrews. The Museums' collection of thumbscrews shows a variety of designs but the commonest were those where pressure was applied by turning a winged nut. Although the use of thumbscrews is recorded throughout the 16th century, linked to a variety of crimes, their application is more generally associated, in the 17th century,

Thumbscrews, manacles, handcuffs and jougs, 17th and 18th century.

The Maiden in use: a mid-19th-century interpretation from the scrapbook of Daniel Wilson.

with the suppression of the Covenanters during the reign of Charles II.

Witchcraft seized the popular imagination in the 16th century and sporadic purges continued in Scotland into the 17th century. Suspects were often gagged with branks, an iron framework which fitted into the mouth to compress the tongue, and the Museums have a large collection of these 'Scold's Bridles'.

The ultimate sentence imposed by the courts for a criminal offence was death. Execution, depending on the seriousness of the offence, was by hanging, drowning, burning, or beheading by the Maiden. Constructed in 1564 at the command of the Provost and Magistrates of Edinburgh who were probably influenced by the beheading machines used both on the Continent and at Halifax, the Maiden replaced the 'heiding sword', and was in use for 150 years. During this time some one hundred men and women were executed, the victims including people from all ranks of society guilty of such crimes as theft, poisoning, murder, piracy and treason. The Maiden

ceased to be used in 1710, and was donated to the Museum in 1797.

Iron age horse furniture

From at least the early bronze age the horse appears to have been an admired and prestigious beast. By the iron age functional items of horse furniture, the buckles, bridle bits, cheekpieces, linchpins and terrets needed to harness and control a horse, were being made of cast bronze and had become highly decorative. A number of single horse bronzes have been found; some of these may have been lost by their owners while others were deliberately buried in hoards. Within the national collections there are examples of horse furniture derived from both hoards and random finds and dating from the 3rd century BC to the 3rd century AD.

Undoubtedly the most remarkable item of horse furniture is the pony cap from Torrs Farm, Kelton, Kirkcudbright. This unique piece, the entire surface of

Pony cap from Torrs, Kirkcudbrightshire, 3rd century BC: a 19th-century
reconstruction which has mistakenly
joined drinking-horn terminals to the
original pony cap.

which is decorated with fine repoussé work (designs in
hammered relief), was found around 1820 in association
with two fine curving drinking horn terminals. These
horns and the cap were originally interpreted as a cham-
frain used to mask the eyes and face of a pony, and in
a reconstruction the drinking horn terminals were posi-
tioned to protrude from the supposed forehead of the
beast. In fact it is more likely that this was a decorative
cap worn on top of the pony's head, the apparent 'eye-
holes' being openings for the animal's ears. The highly
appealing design on this cap has a prime place in the
sequence of artistic development in Celtic Britain, and
has been dated on stylistic grounds to the latter part of
the 3rd century BC.

A more typical hoard containing horse furniture was
found in 1737 in a moss near Middlebie, Dumfriesshire.
Twenty-eight items were recovered, all but four dress
fasteners and a sword hilt guard being parts of horse
harness, including bridle bits, cheek rings, strap junctions
and terrets. Among the most striking of the isolated finds
is the intact bridle bit with decorative enamel work discovered before 1785 in the bottom of a moss at the end of

Birrenswark hillfort, Dumfriesshire. There is evidence of
both pre-Roman and Roman activity at Birrenswark hillfort and the bridle bit probably dates from the mid-1st
century AD. Another remarkable piece of horse furniture is
the elongated strap junction made of cast bronze and decorated with red, blue and white enamel from the Roman
fortress of Inchtuthill, Perthshire. The pristine condition
of this piece suggests that it was little used and it is
likely to date to the brief life of the fortress, from 83/4
to 87/90 AD.

Iron age jewellery

Before the arrival of the Roman forces in 80 AD, a flourishing native jewellery industry existed, producing items,
now in the national collections, such as the gold–
silver alloy torc found at New Cairnmuir, Peeblesshire,
the bronze hinged armlet from Plunton Castle, Kirkcudbrightshire, and the sheet bronze collar found at
Stitchill, Roxburghshire.

The appearance of alien forms resulted in a remarkable cross-fertilization, and the Scottish jewellery

Hinged bronze collar from Stitchell,
Roxburghshire, 1st century AD.

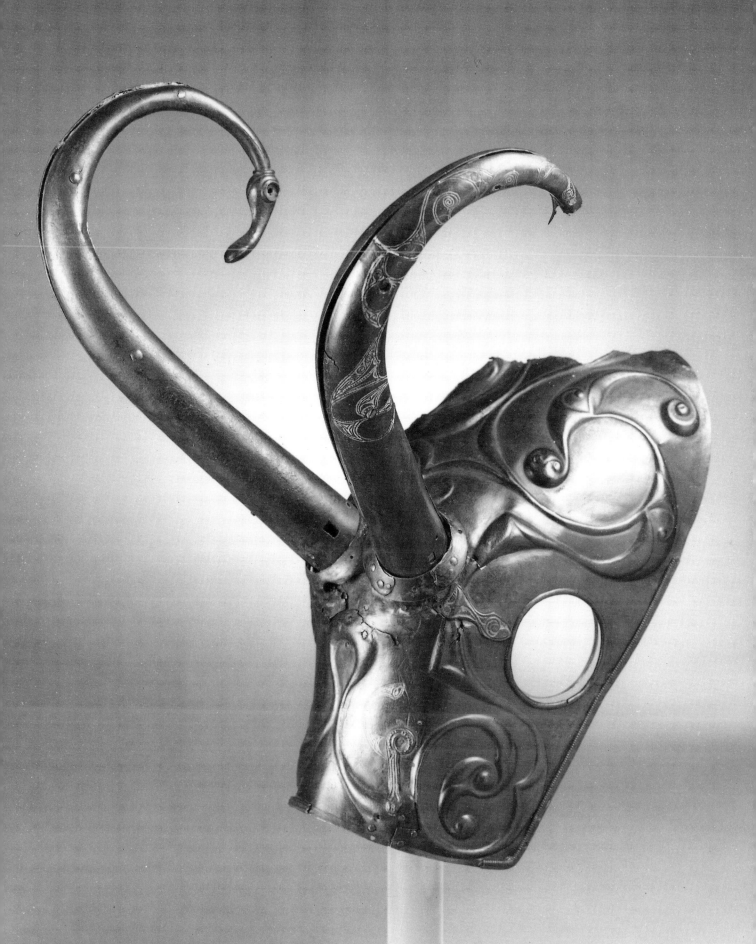

of the first three centuries AD represents a combination, in varying degrees, of the native and Roman traditions. Purely Roman items in the collections are represented by such pieces as the imported Rhenish swastika brooch from Denholm Farm, Roxburghshire, and the cock-shaped brooch from Bow Broch, Midlothian, whilst the native tradition is shown in the 'dragonesque' brooches from Newstead, Roxburghshire, and by the frequent use of enamelwork. Other items, such as penannular and trumpet-shaped brooches, represent the products of one tradition which were adopted and adapted by people accustomed to another tradition.

The range of items used as jewellery during these centuries comprises brooches and pins, neck ornaments (torcs, collars and bead necklaces), bangles and armlets (see **Massive and snake armlets**), pendants and finger rings. The sheet-bronze mirror from Balmaclellan, Kirkcudbrightshire, another product of the native metalwork industry, should also be mentioned in this context.

The material most commonly used for these items is bronze, usually in the form of cast bronze. Items were often embellished with enamel inlays of various colours (red, blue, yellow and green) which were used either singly or in two-colour combinations. An imported Gallo-Roman brooch from Carlungie, Angus, has the additional feature of inlaid glass panels. Other metals were occasionally used: a silver trumpet brooch is known from Ayrshire, and a gold–silver alloy (electrum) was used for the New Cairnmuir torc. Glass also features, in the manufacture of bangles and beads, and once more a variety of colours is found. Opaque blue and yellow appear to have been the most popular.

Whilst the larger and more precious pieces of jewellery would have been reserved for the higher echelons of native and Romano-British society, items such as brooches and beads would probably have had wider currency. It is clear that both sexes wore jewellery, and contemporary Roman sculpture gives us some insights into the way it would have been worn: many brooches, for instance, would have been pinned to the shoulder or upper chest part of a tunic.

Iron age warfare

Classical authors' descriptions suggest that Celtic warfare was as much about display and noise as it was about combat. That martial prowess was a matter for great esteem and conferred high social status can be deduced from the surviving Irish epics, which reflect an earlier Celtic world. Nevertheless, the archaeological evidence for warfare between groups in Britain is sparse. Although the landscape is full of the remains of defended hill-top enclosures, many of which were occupied and used during the second half of the first millennium BC, the evidence for actual attacks on them is virtually non-existent before the arrival of the Roman armies.

In Scotland the presence of numerous hillforts and other defensive structures is the most powerful indicator of the threats posed by raiding and warfare. The actual weapons used on such occasions are very much rarer.

The commonest weapons were the sword and the spear. No definitely pre-Roman swords survive from Scotland. Three reasonably complete swords, all in the national collections, have been found at the Roman forts of Fendoch, Perthshire, and Newstead, Roxburghshire, probably the weapons of native troops serving with the Roman army. Otherwise, the existence of swords is more commonly recognized by surviving scabbard fittings. The remarkable metal scabbard from Mortonhall, Midlothian, shows the quality of craftsmanship devoted to weapons at this period. Spears are even less well represented with the most distinctive find being the metal butts mounted at the end of the shaft to counterbalance the weight of the head.

Shields are similarly rare although the presence of several native warriors with them on the Bridgeness slab (see **Roman stone sculpture**) suggests that they were relatively common. Two iron bosses were found in the Roman-period hoards from Blackburn Mill, Berwickshire, and Carlingwark, Kirkcudbrightshire, and the decorated strips from the hoard found at Balmaclellan, Dumfriesshire have been interpreted as decorative mountings for a wooden shield. But these are the only Scottish finds.

Display and noise involved major items of equipment: the chariot and the carnyx or war-trumpet. Convincing evidence for chariots is lacking (see **Iron age horse furniture**) but the head of a carnyx was found at Deskford, Banffshire. This is the only surviving carnyx from Britain and one of only three known from Europe. It is made of sheet bronze in the form of a boar's head. The noise from these trumpets was intended to frighten and confuse the enemy.

Iron and steel
see **Coal, oil and the metals**

Ironwork
see **Architectural ironwork; Domestic metalwork**

Jet necklaces

Elaborate 'spacer-plate' jet necklaces, and plainer neck-laces of washer- and barrel-shaped jet beads, were used as valuable and prestigious items of jewellery in Britain and Ireland during the early bronze age (around 2000–1600 BC). About half of the surviving examples are in the national collections.

'Spacer-plate' necklaces consist of numerous plain, barrel-shaped beads (a complete example from Balcalk, Angus, has 140), together with a triangular toggle, two roughly triangular end plates, and four roughly rect-angular or trapeze-shaped spacer plates. The end and spacer plates are sometimes decorated on the outside with dot-punched designs, reminiscent of those found on contemporary pottery. The fibre used for stringing the beads does not usually survive.

The function of the spacer plates is to enable the stringing of increasing numbers of beads from the back to the front of the necklace to create a crescent shape. To this end, the interior of each plate has been bored in a series of Y shapes, so that the number of strings attach-ing to the plate may increase from, say, four to seven. Nineteenth- and 20th-century reconstructions of such necklaces are often erroneous, reflecting the archaeologist's preconceptions about style. It is most likely that the beads at the front of the necklace were arranged in plain strands, graded by size of bead from small at the top to large at the bottom.

The plainer necklaces consist of washer-shaped beads, or varying combinations of washer- and barrel-shaped beads, sometimes with a triangular toggle. Rare complete examples have between about 160 and 210 beads. These necklaces are probably broadly contemporary with spacer-plate necklaces, being found in similar contexts and with similar associated material.

Jet necklaces are most commonly found in graves, and although they tend to be associated with female burials, male associations are not unknown (eg Knockenny, Angus). Their relative scarcity as grave goods suggests

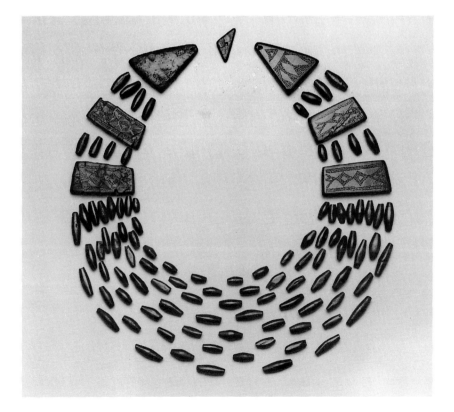

Jet spacer-plate necklace from Mount Stuart, Bute, 2000–1600 BC. This picture shows how the spacer plates and jet beads may have been arranged.

Orkney and Shetland Breed, oil painting by William Shiels, about 1835. **Man and beast**

that their wearers were accorded special status; and the condition of several necklaces indicates that they had been worn for some time before burial. Occasionally token fragments of necklaces are found in graves, and in at least one case a plate from a second necklace has been inserted, perhaps to replace a missing piece.

Spacer-plate necklaces are closely comparable with gold lunulae (see **Bronze age goldwork**), and may well have developed from them. Contemporary versions of spacer-plate necklaces in amber are also known, from rich tombs in Wessex and Mycenae. An important associated piece is the fragmentary amber necklace from the Knowes of Trotty, Orkney. A bronze piece amongst a hoard from Migdale, Sutherland is also possibly related; and bronze armlets from Melfort, Argyll, and Masterton, Fife, bear repoussé decoration reminiscent of barrel-shaped beads.

Although varying degrees of skill are displayed in their manufacture, the jet necklaces appear to have been made by specialist craftspeople. The technology for working and decorating jet artefacts was simple, requiring only a knife, rubbing stone and flint or metal borers. The source of the jet is assumed to be Whitby in Yorkshire, but four Scottish sources also exist. It is not known whether the latter were exploited.

Jewellery
see **Commemorative jewellery; Gems; Heart brooches; Iron age jewellery; Jet necklaces; Massive and snake armlets; Medieval and Renaissance jewellery; Military orders, decorations and medals; Pseudo-penannular brooches; Ring brooches; Viking goldwork**

Knitting
see **Textiles**

Lace
see **Textiles**

Leather-worker's tool box

This remarkable leather-worker's tool box was found in 1885 by men cutting peat on an isolated stretch of ground belonging to the farm of Howe, Evie, Orkney. The box itself is the only known example of decorated wood carving from Scotland of the 7th to 10th century AD.

The box is carved from a single piece of alder. Two long sides and one end are decorated with complex

Box from Evie, Orkney, 8th–10th century AD, which contained the surviving handles of what were probably a leatherworker's tools.

Head of a bronze war trumpet (originally about 2 m long) in the form of a boar's head, from Deskford, Banffshire, 1st century BC – 1st century AD. **Iron age warfare**

Monart Vasart glass, Perth, 1924 to about 1950. **Glass**

Lamps and candlesticks with *foreground* tinderbox, flint and steel, and fir splints, 18th and 19th century. **Lighting**

Instruments from the Adie workshop,
Edinburgh: mine surveyor's dial, 1830,
reflecting microscope, about 1830, short
beam balance, about 1855, theodolite,
about 1875. **History of physical science**

Lighthouse optic designed by Thomas
Stevenson, 1866, used to guide
shipping into the River Tay.
Lighthouses

Battle axes, 2000–1500 BC, from
Pentland, Midlothian *left*, Burnside Mill,
Angus and Portpatrick, Wigtownshire
right. **Maceheads, battleaxes and
hammers**

Model of the Bell Rock lighthouse at low
tide, made for Robert Stevenson in 1822.

curvilinear motifs. Its sliding lid survives only as dis-
torted shrunken fragments. The decoration on the lid is
similar to that on the rest of the box. This decoration is
closely paralleled on the large sculptured stones of the
same date and in surviving manuscripts such as the
Books of Kells and Durrow.

A collection of objects was found within the box.
There were seven wooden, four bone and three horn
handles. The metal tools to which these had been fitted
had all been destroyed by corrosion. In addition, an
antler peg, parts of three tines and a roughly rectangular
strip of cut antler were recovered. The group is completed by a lump of pumice, rubbed smooth, and a small
part of a leather strap. The size and shape of these
handles and tools suggest that they constitute a leather-
worker's kit.

Lighthouses

The expansion of Scotland's overseas trade during the
early 17th century emphasized the fact that the country

has an inhospitable coast line. In 1635 a Crown patent
was granted for the erection of a fire beacon on the Isle of
May, with shipping passing the Firth of Forth paying a
toll to the proprietors. In 1687 the Fraternity of Masters
and Seamen of Dundee erected leading lights to mark the
mouth of the Tay. In the 18th century, with the growth
of trade to North America, civic authorities on the west
coast took action to help vessels find their ports; the
town of Dumfries erected a lighthouse at Southerness in
1748 and in 1757 the mouth of the Clyde was marked by
beacons erected by a public trust.

In 1786, stimulated by the massive loss of shipping
during storms which had struck the Scottish coasts in
1782, the government established the Northern Lighthouse Board, with the remit to erect lighthouses at
Kinnaird Head, North Ronaldsay, Eilean Glas and the
Mull of Kintyre. This work was completed in under
three years and such was the praise received from mariners
that under a new act of 1789 the Board was required 'to
cause such other lighthouses to be erected upon any parts
of the coast of Scotland as they shall deem necessary'.

The success with which the Board provided beacons to guide the mariner around the coast of Scotland (and from 1815 the Isle of Man) can be attributed to the energy and engineering skills of Thomas Smith, engineer to the Board from 1786 until about 1806, his successor and son-in-law Robert Stevenson (1772–1850) and Robert's sons David (1815–86) and Thomas (1818–87).

The Museums hold an extensive collection of historic lighthouse material, the bulk of which has been deposited by the Northern Lighthouse Board. Lamps include an 1810 Argand burner, an early electric arc lamp of 1886, petroleum vapour lamps and incandescent electric lamps. There is an early faceted reflector of the type first installed by Thomas Smith, and an improved parabolic reflector as introduced by Robert Stevenson in 1810. Most impressive are the glass optical systems on the Fresnel pattern copied from the French and introduced at Inchkeith in 1835. That optic, together with its replacement and the revolving apparatus used at Inchkeith from 1889 until 1983, are in the collection. There are also examples of the first holophote lenses, developed by Thomas Stevenson in the 1840s.

Lighthouses themselves are, perforce, represented by models. The model of the Bell Rock is that commissioned by Robert Stevenson in 1822. It is particularly interesting because it shows the temporary accommodation platform built for the workmen, and some of the other equipment used during the three years of construction, 1807 to 1810.

The most recent acquisition is the lantern-housing erected at Girdle Ness in 1833. This is of the pattern first used by Smith and Stevenson, but replaced as improved optics were installed later in the 19th century. Girdle Ness was upgraded in 1847; however, the old lantern was not scrapped but taken to Inchkeith and used to house experimental optics. Rediscovered in 1985, the iron framework of the lantern has been restored, revealing a series of decorative panels, apparently symbolic of the work of the Northern Lighthouse Board in making navigation safe around the hazardous coasts of Scotland.

Lighting

Lighting was not a reliable form of illumination until the invention of pressure oil lamps in the 19th century. There was then lighting by gas, and subsequently by electricity. The collections of the National Museums include examples of each stage in the progression of methods of lighting from the primitive to the sophisticated.

Brass cruisie lamp, 18th century.

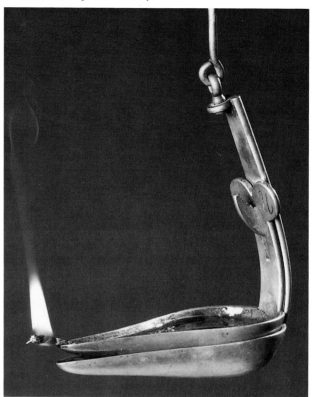

The commonest method of making fire and light was by striking a flint with a piece of steel, known in the past as a 'fleerish'. This took many forms and was made by the blacksmith to be decorative as well as useful. This lighting device of flint and steel was usually kept in a container with tinder which was any dry and inflammable substance. The tinder box was often well made and lavished with an artistic finish.

Candles were another source of light. These were made from tallow, a form of coarse, hard fat derived from animals – sheep, cattle or wild deer – which was melted down into moulds. Holders for candles took many forms, both plain and decorative, and were made in a variety of different metals, both precious and base. The possession of candlesticks was, in the medieval period, a symbol of wealth and status.

Those without the resources to make candles, for whom animals were too valuable to kill in quantity, used other forms of lighting such as 'candles' of fir or splints of bog wood. These would burn, if only for a short time, with surprising intensity of light. There was a tradition that the 'puir man' or vagrant would hold the splint for a light for the family at their domestic tasks; this gave rise to the name 'puir man' or 'peerman' for the wrought-iron light holder or bracket made by the blacksmith.

The blacksmith-made iron cruisie was a form of hanging oil lamp in universal use in Scotland until the 19th century and in remote areas into the 20th century. Its shape is so like that of a Roman hanging lamp that it was probably modelled on it. The Scottish cruisie has two pans, the upper for the oil and wick, and the lower to catch the dripping fuel. The oil was made in the home, from tallow in inland communities and from fish livers in coastal communities.

Linen
see **Textiles**

Luckenbooth brooches
see **Heart brooches**

Maceheads, battle axes and axe hammers

A tradition of using hafted pieces of visually attractive, shaped stone as symbols of power is in evidence in Britain and Ireland from around 3000 BC to around 1500 BC. The earlier forms of such items are called maceheads, whilst the later forms are known as battle axes. So-called axe hammers resemble workaday versions of battle axes, and were used for utilitarian rather than ceremonial purposes (although not necessarily for the functions indicated by their name). The holdings of the National Museums form one of the finest collections of maceheads, battle axes and axe hammers in Britain and Ireland, and comprise a large proportion of the Scottish specimens.

The maceheads dating to the Neolithic period (down to about 2500 BC) can be divided into two basic forms: pestle- and egg-shaped. Both are characterized by the use of distinctive stone types, such as richly coloured flint or speckled amphibolite, and both represent a considerable input of time and specialist skill. The stone types used are particularly hard, and it is notoriously difficult to bore a cylindrical hole through a block of flint.

One sub-group of egg-shaped maceheads, the so-called 'Maesmore' type, displays even greater virtuosity in its manufacture, as these items have ground and polished designs, usually of interlocking diamond shapes. The specimen from Airdens, Sutherland, is a good example. These Maesmore-type maceheads are comparable in their overall design to contemporary carved stone balls.

Maceheads are commonly but not exclusively found in funerary contexts, and there is a remarkable concentration of both pestle- and egg-shaped specimens in the Orkney Islands. A third type, the 'cushion' macehead, which apparently dates to around 2500 BC, also clusters in the Orkney islands.

Numerous variants of battle axes have been identified, and a detailed developmental scheme covering their period of use from 2000 BC to 1500 BC has been worked out, but the basic design is that of a weapon-like object, with one sharp end and one blunt end. The battle axe from Broomend of Crichie, Aberdeenshire, has a 'waisted' form, with the added feature of incised lines. Hard and often visually striking stone was used for these artefacts, and recent work on Scottish specimens suggests that locally available cobbles were utilized. The task of battle axe manufacture is estimated to have taken at least 25 hours: three to four for pecking out the rough shape, three for grinding it smooth, 15 to 20 for drilling the shafthole, and the remainder for polishing.

A very rare faceted stone macehead from Airdens, Sutherland, around 3000 BC.

Axe hammers resemble unpolished versions of battle axes, but differ in several respects, namely size (axe hammers tend to be over 7 in (18 cm), long, battle axes under 7 in (18 cm), findspot type (battle axes are usually found in graves, axe hammers never so) and distribution (battle axes are spread thinly throughout southern and central Scotland, axe hammers cluster in the south-west). However, the same rock types are used for their manufacture. It has recently been suggested that they may have been used as tips for ards (early ploughs).

Machine tools
see Engineering

Man and beast

On first sight it may appear that animal husbandry has continued much as in the past, but with the addition of vastly improved veterinary knowledge, the convenience of milking machines and bulk transport, and the latter-day developments of intensive production. However, there is more to it than that. The relationship between people and animals has changed as part of the move from subsistence to industrialized agriculture. This involves a shift of emphasis from keeping animals for their 'live' produce of milk and wool, and strength in the plough or pack harness, to treating the animals as more of a finite crop. Material in the National Museums reflects this changing relationship.

Before the 18th century cattle rather than horses were the mainstay of cultivation, particularly in the Lowlands. Because the old-style ox and horse harness was home-made and not durable, little survives, although the collection does contain rare examples of ox harness used in the transitional stages to horse power. However, with the spread of the Clydesdale breed of horse in the late 18th century, solid saddler-made graith (gear) was needed to harness its strength, and examples from the 19th century onwards of plough, cart and show harness are well represented.

However, one important category of early horse gear survives in some detail: pack harness, and with it, the slypes, sledge-like vehicles, that preceded wheeled transport. Associated with this are a variety of creels and straw containers.

The Clydesdale was one among many animal breeds that became identified with improved farming. The great experimental period of animal breeding from the late 18th to the mid-19th century is summed up in the superb collection of animal portraits, painted by William Shiels for Professor David Low's work on British domestic breeds. Low recorded the then old as well as the new, and since both breeding and genetic drift have changed the breeds further this record is invaluable, and is being augmented by further acquisition.

The animal portraits illustrate a watershed between the more general-purpose breeds of the old-style farming and the trend to beef or dairy specialization which increasingly differentiated cattle beasts in improved farming. The contents of the milk house have been collected in some detail, not only the hand equipment for butter- and cheese-making, but also early milking machinery in the development of which Scotland was in the forefront.

Although the small and hardy fine-woolled breeds of sheep gave way to the coarser and harder-woolled but more productive breeds of Cheviot and Blackface from the 18th century onwards, the traditions of sheep husbandry have more continuity than other branches of farming. Besides the artefacts which reflect this continuity are those that represent an enormous change in animal husbandry in general: veterinary equipment. This is complemented by equally fascinating relics of the older world of charms and superstition used to counter animal ills (see **Charms and amulets**).

Linked with sheep husbandry is the whole range of equipment associated with textiles, from the cards used to prepare fibres for spinning to the looms for weaving it. Whether for wool or lint, the range of processing equipment is detailed and comprehensive, and a very important record of an activity that is Scotland's oldest commercial enterprise (see **Rural homes; Textile, paper and printing industries**).

The most drastic change in the management of animals effected by farming improvement was the substitution of naturally regenerating grass by sown fodder crops. In time this change led to the production of a whole range of specialized equipment, for hay, turnips and potatoes. The importance of these was enhanced as the latter two crops were increasingly used to feed humans as well as animals. So fundamental is this to improved agriculture that collecting in this section has been thorough and comprehensive, from drill ploughs to the first effective potato harvesters complete with electronic sensors.

If the opposite of living off animals' labour and products is direct consumption, that is represented by two contrasting activities: poaching and pig killing. Poaching is an unorthodox branch of the hunting tradition but nevertheless part of country life. The collection reflects not only illegal ingenuity, but also the counter-offensive man traps and scare guns. There is also the normal equipment of the gamekeeper, mole- and rabbit-catcher. Keeping pigs is a legal facet of the same phenomenon – the purpose of keeping the animals can only be realized by killing them. Pig-killing equipment is well represented.

Between the wild and domesticated is the world of the bee. Honey was once the only common source of sweetening. The artefacts of bee-keeping have been collected in some detail, reflecting the skill of country people in developing bee-keeping to its present level.

Ploughman and pair of horse in cart harness at Coldstream Carluke, Lanarkshire, probably 1920s. *(Mrs Graham, Linlithgow; SEA)*

Marine engineering
see **Ships and marine engineering**

Massive and snake armlets

Massive and snake armlets are distinctively Scottish. There is a clear relationship between them in terms of design solutions and shared motifs, and in distribution which is concentrated in eastern Scotland south of the Moray Firth. Both types of armlet seem to date from the first centuries

AD although the evidence for dating is not strong. Collectively, they represent outstanding examples of iron age bronzeworking.

Just over 20 massive armlets, so called because of their weight and overall dimensions, are known although five of these have been lost. Half the surviving examples are in the national collections. The only find from outside Scotland is one from Newry, Co. Down, Ireland, but this is clearly a Scottish product. The characteristic form is a penannular armlet with expanded perforated terminals. In a small number of examples, all in the British Museum, London, these perforations are filled by enamelled discs. The armlets often, though not invariably, occur as pairs. Their considerable size and weight raises the possibility that they were not for personal use but formed instead decorative pieces for greater-than-life-size wooden statues which have not survived.

A smaller number of snake armlets have been found. Eight have snake-headed terminals but in four other cases the head has been replaced by a knob. All but one from a burial at Snailwell, Cambridgeshire, were found in Scotland. With the exception of the Snailwell example they are all in the national collections. As the name suggests these are spiral armlets with snake's heads and bodies, albeit somewhat stylistically treated. On no good evidence the Snailwell armlet has been assumed to be the prototype for the group, but it seems more likely that snake armlets are an indigenous development.

Mathematics
see **Applied mathematics**

Medals
see also **Military orders, decorations and medals**

Commemorative coin-like discs struck in bronze, silver or gold are known from the Classical civilizations of Greece and Rome in which they performed the diplomatic and even poetic function of reminding citizens of

Snake armlet from Culbin Sands, Morayshire, 1st–2nd century AD.

the greatness of emperors, feats of arms and significant achievements. The medal as a work of art reappeared in 15th-century Italy whose school of medallists inspired similar schools in Germany later in the century, followed by others elsewhere in northern Europe.

The arts and tastes of the Renaissance ensured that medals were more highly decorated than coins and a focus of portraiture, allegory and symbolism, combined with political commentary. Typically, the obverse or 'heads' side of the medal would present a portrait of the monarch, leader or patron, and the reverse or 'tails' side would celebrate his power or action and, symbolically, reveal more of the sitter's personality. The scope of the medallist's art was extended in the 16th-century when propaganda was added to eulogistic portraiture.

Few early medals survive in Scotland. An exception, now in the National Museums, is the medal dated 1491 of William Scheves, James III's Archbishop of St Andrews. Scheves was an outstanding example of a new breed of royal servant, essentially a politician and diplomat rather than an ecclesiastic, for whom the medallion portrait represented essential political hard currency.

After the Reformation the affairs of church were added to the affairs of state as suitable subjects for glorification as well as for satire, ridicule and humiliation. Medals, both official and unofficial, constitute an intimate commentary on the events which they commemorated. Typical of these in the National Museums is the gold medal commemorating the marriage of James VI to the young princess, Anne of Denmark, in Oslo in 1589. The medal is of international political significance, marking a diplomatic triumph for the Protestant party in the face of Catholic counter-Reformation.

As documents and mirrors of history, the Museums' pro- and anti-Jacobite medals represent a subtle commentary on their times; the early 18th-century anti-Jacobite medals for example reflect the considerable contemporary anxiety for the security of the nation and for the recently established Hanoverian monarchy.

The improvement of minting machinery during the

Medals of the 15th and 16th centuries, including Archbishop Scheves medal *top* and James VI marriage medal *bottom*.

Industrial Revolution produced a flood of medals as prizes and awards of merit, and a new generation of British medallists and engravers who worked almost entirely in the neo-classical style. The collections include a large number of prize medals awarded by improving societies such as the Highland and Agricultural Society of Scotland. It was not until the end of the 19th century that a new interest in medallic art broke the moulds of convention in favour of the freer styles of contemporary art nouveau painting and sculpture, and the use of a variety of forms other than the traditional disc.

Medieval and Renaissance jewellery
see also **Heart brooches; Ring brooches**

The National Museums have a collection of several hundred pieces of jewellery dating from the 12th to the 16th century. Many of these are ring brooches described separately.

Several finger rings also survive from the medieval period, some set with precious stones. Two 13th-century examples were found with a hoard of coins and other jewellery at Canonbie in Dumfriesshire. One has a garnet, the other a sapphire surrounded by six emerald sparks. Other rings have inscriptions, religious images or merchants' marks. A favourite was the 'fede' ring with a bezel in the form of clasped hands, and in others the bezel could

Jewellery, 13th to 15th century: *left to right* 'fede' ring, two rings from Canonbie, crucifix from Craigmillar Castle and a cross from Threave Castle.

serve as a seal. The few other items of medieval jewellery include a silver-gilt reliquary cross from Threave Castle, Kirkcudbrightshire, and a silver rosary crucifix of similar date from Craigmillar Castle.

From the second half of the 16th century there is a small group of important jewellery of Scottish manufacture, including two pieces associated with Mary, Queen of Scots. One is the locket from the Penicuik Jewels which is said to have been a gift from the Queen to her servant Giles Mowbray just before her death. It is gold, enamelled with a surround of seed pearls and has thumb nail paintings of a man and a woman. There are other lockets of this type, including another two in the Museums. In a similar style is a heart-shaped gold enamelled pendant which contains a French cameo of Mary, Queen of Scots and its original mounting. The cameo may have been a present from Mary to one of her supporters.

Memorabilia

Objects associated with characters from Scotland's past hold a certain fascination. Sometimes they may be linked to a romantic figure or period, for example, the numerous reputed relics of the Jacobite cause, or they may have a more sinister aspect as with the lamp and keys of Deacon William Brodie, cabinet-maker and respected Edinburgh citizen by day, housebreaker by night.

Among the most unusual relics held in the Museums is the mask, wig and dagger of the Covenanting minister, Alexander Peden. Peden, who was from Ayrshire, wore the mask and wig, from about 1660 to 1670 to prevent recognition while travelling round Scotland and while preaching at the banned conventicles or open-air services which were a feature of the Covenanting period in the 1660s and 70s.

Other interesting relics include a coconut cup and sea chest of Alexander Selkirk, who was originally from Largo in Fife. Selkirk's adventures became the basis for Daniel Defoe's *Robinson Crusoe*. Put ashore on the island of Juan Fernandez after quarrelling with the ship's captain, Selkirk remained on the island from 1704 to 1709.

Many objects have, over the years, acquired doubtful associations with the ill-fated Jacobite cause. A knife, fork and spoon recently purchased by the Museums, however, have a strong provenance. Originally made in Paris about 1738–40, the cutlery was possibly bought by Ranald MacDonald, younger of Clanranald. His father, also Ranald, presented Prince Charles Edward Stuart with a silver 'cover', probably the cutlery, in 1746 following

Lantern and skeleton keys used in
evidence at the trial of Deacon William
Brodie, 1788.

the defeat at Culloden. Some six weeks later the Prince
gave the knife, fork and spoon to Murdoch Macleod,
one of his companions, and these items have descended
directly through the family until they were acquired by
the Museums.

Metal
see Coal, oil and the metals

Metalwork
see Bronze age sheet metalwork;
Domestic metalwork

Meteorites

The study of meteorites reveals information about solar
system processes and they have therefore been investigated
by astronomers, physicists, chemists and geologists. There
are many reasons for supposing that the matter deep in the
earth's interior is very different from surface rocks. Since
direct observation of deep levels is impossible, meteorites
are of great scientific interest for the window they open
into the great depth of the earth. In addition, meteorites
are the only tangible objects of the universe beyond our
star–planet–moon system.

Meteorites are classified into three major groups: stony
(chondrites), irons (which contain mostly iron and nickel),
and stony-irons (a mixture). Chondrites constitute the
largest group, accounting for 70 per cent of all falls.

Approximately 2600 falls throughout the world (excluding
Antarctica) are documented; of 21 recorded from the
British Isles, three fell on Scotland. A fourth record, the
Tiree meteorite of about 1808, is of doubtful status. The
three Scottish meteorites are named after the localities in
which they fell: High Possil, near Glasgow, which fell in
1804, Perth (1830) and Strathmore, Perthshire (1917). All
are stony meteorites and only small fragments of the High
Possil and Perth stones were recovered. The High Possil
meteorite produced, according to one eyewitness, a trail
of smoke, whereas the Strathmore meteorite generated
a brilliant fireball travelling from the south-east to the
north-west over Perthshire. After a loud detonation from
the latter meteorite four stones were recovered, each stone
being named after the locality in which it landed: Easter
Essendy, Carsie, Keithick and Corston. The largest
fragment, Easter Essendy, weighing about 22 lb (10.1 kg)
and the Keithick stone are in the national collections.

Meteorology
see also **History of physical science**

The earliest instrument in the national collections is an
example of the first successful thermometer. It dates from
about 1660 and was made for the Academia del Cimento
in Florence. A cache of these spirit of wine instruments
was discovered in Florence in the 19th century, and a few
were given to notable overseas scientists–in this instance
to J D Forbes, professor of Natural Philosophy in the
University of Edinburgh.

The largest group of meteorological instruments are
barometers, the majority being domestic barometers, items
of furniture rather than scientific instruments. The work
of Balthazar Knie, a German immigrant who settled in
Edinburgh in the 1770s, stands out. Technically interesting
is an early 19th-century mountain barometer by Miller
and Adie of Edinburgh, for use in estimating altitude by

Small glass decanter used by officers of the 94th, Scotch Brigade, about 1810, probably in the field.

measuring pressure differences. There are a number of examples of the 'sympiesometer', patented by Alexander Adie in 1818, and widely used until the invention of the aneroid barometer.

From the collections of the Scottish Meteorological Society came an example of the anemometer or wind gauge, made by Adie in the early 19th century to the 1775 design of the Edinburgh physician James Lind (1736–1812).

Military art

The Scottish United Services Museum houses a growing collection of material in the categories of fine and decorative art. The fine art includes oil paintings, watercolours, prints and photographs, while gold, silver, ceramics and glass feature in the decorative art collections.

From the late 18th to the early 20th century there was considerable popular interest in Britain's naval and armed forces. The interest intensified in proportion to colonial expansion and martial struggle, until the jingoism of the South African War. Sufficient momentum survived to fuel initial popular enthusiasm for the First World War.

Before the advent of television, public visual imagery was created by artists working for illustrated books and magazines or by painters producing large-scale canvases devoted to historical and contemporary incidents in war. The greatest exponents of this new *oeuvre* were the French. Britain had a group of competent painters, the finest being Elizabeth, Lady Butler, whose *Scotland For Ever* is one of the most memorable of 19th-century battle series. It depicts a charge by the only Scottish cavalry regiment, the Royal Scots Greys, during the Battle of Waterloo. Robert Gibb RSA (1845–1932) was the best Scottish exponent of battle painting and his *Hougoumont* of 1903 is in the collection. It, too, depicts an incident at Waterloo.

Watercolourists also chose marine and military subjects, particularly uniform, though they too depicted historical and contemporary battle scenes. The collection concentrates on Scots who worked in this medium and there is a good representative selection of work by William Skeoch Cumming (1864–1929). He exploited photography as a painting aid.

The large collection of prints is mainly devoted to the development of uniform but does contain many portraits of leading military and naval commanders. The print was the cheapest form of visual image for the greater part of the 19th century and various methods of reproduction were invented to allow fast, coloured pictures to be produced to satisfy demand.

Anemometer, Lind pressure tube wind gauge, made by Adie & Son, Edinburgh, about 1855.

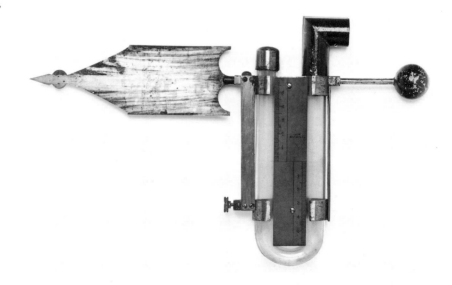

Far right Piper Muir of the Black Watch, 1856.

'Jingling Johnny' or *çaghana* of Turkish origin, about 1805, of the 3rd Regiment of Foot Guards (now the Scots Guards).

Until the invention of the half-tone block, photographs could not be reproduced in the same number as lithographic prints which had the additional attraction of colour, but the accuracy and immediacy of the photograph was in the end to supersede the hand-drawn image. The Museums hold a major collection of glass negatives portraying the Household Division of the British Army.

Gold and silver were used for presentation and commemorative pieces given to individuals and regiments. Freedom of a city or burgh was often given in a gold or silver box which could then be used to contain snuff. Plate, suitably inscribed, was awarded as prizes or gifts within regiments. Wealthy regiments gradually acquired considerable collections of silver as a result, which was normally displayed in the officers' mess. To this day, individual regiments commission complete sets of tableware or mark anniversaries and special occasions by purchasing a piece of silver.

Volunteer units were often staffed by wealthy landowners and professional men who presented pieces of silver to their regiments. These appear occasionally at auction and the Museum has been able to add examples to the collection.

Another group of specialist objects can be included in the precious metals category. These are early breast Stars of various chivalric orders, often of excellent workmanship and manufactured from gold and silver with elaborate enamel work. Firms such as Rundell, Bridge and Rundell, Jefferys and Wirgman (all of London) produced both British and foreign insignia of the highest quality. Apart from pieces by these firms, the National Museums' collection of insignia contains work by the firm of Hamilton & Company, based in Calcutta during the British administration of India.

Military music

Music for the serviceman helped to build morale and maintain it in battles and on the march. It discouraged and was popularly believed to demoralize the enemy and, most importantly, for an age without electronic signalling or telephones, it provided signals in barracks, camp and field. The bugle or trumpet call fulfilled, for servicemen without watches, much the same purpose as the factory hooter.

Woodwind, brass and percussion instruments are the only types which can satisfactorily be played on the march. Thus, bands incorporating such instrumentation developed in the British Army and became known as military bands. However, not all military music is performed by military bands and other groups of musicians have a place in the world of the serviceman and woman.

Fifes and Drums, known today as Corps of Drums, date from 1660 within the British Army but are now restricted to the regiments of Foot Guards and of English line infantry. The fife provided, with or without drums, the greater part of the Army's music for a century or more after 1660. Drums have become symbolic of the British Army and have accompanied it since its earliest days. In battle, instructions to perform complicated deploying manoeuvres would be delivered by drumbeat, the vibrating tones of the rope-tensioned wooden drums being audible for long distances. Drums are usually emblazoned with the insignia and battle honours of their regiment. The Museums' earliest drums and fifes are associated with Scottish auxiliary regiments of the Napoleonic Wars period.

In Scottish regiments establishments of Pipes and Drums (or Drums and Pipes in the unique case of the Gordon

Highlanders) replaced Corps of Drums in the late 19th century. Pipers were first officially authorized for Scottish regiments in 1854 and the pipes and drums concept developed rapidly over the following two decades. However, pipers had existed in Scottish regiments since at least 1684 but, for the next 170 years, their existence was unofficial and their positions funded by the officers of their regiments. Their role was principally that of ordinary soldiers who happened to be pipers. The combined bagpipe collections of the Scottish United Services Museum and the Department of History and Applied Art give the National Museums one of the world's most comprehensive collections of an instrument so emotively associated with Scotland. The Museum's earliest military pipes are a set made for indoor use which would have accompanied the 1st Highland Battalion to America in 1757. (See **Bagpipes**)

Bugles take the place of drums in rifle and light infantry regiments and were used from the foundation of such regiments in the late 18th century to signal orders on the battlefield. Trumpets provided all the 'calls', or signals, and much of the music in the cavalry until the invention of the bugle, which came to be used for calls in the field. The popularity of the Rifle Volunteer movement throughout late 19th-century Britain was particularly marked in Scotland and the Museum possesses an engraved silver

Breast star of a Knight Commander of the Order of the Star of India, 1946.

bugle of the Queen's Edinburgh Rifle Volunteer Brigade dating from 1870 – an instrument typical of those awarded as prizes in such Corps. More recent material, including clarinets and saxophones, reflects the expanded repertoire of the military band.

Military orders, decorations and medals
see also Medals

The military collections of the Scottish United Services Museum contain the National Museums' Collection of Insignia. British and foreign orders of chivalry are represented by awards to Scottish military personnel, many of which reflect alliances with various countries since the beginning of the 19th century.

There is a large collection of campaign medals awarded to Scots, with some gaps representing campaigns where Scots were not involved in large numbers. Privately-issued regimental medals, including examples from militia and volunteer units, are included. The bulk of the collection is devoted to Army awards but there are some awards to men of the Royal Navy and Royal Air Force.

From the mid-17th century until 1725 awards of Orders of Chivalry for military endeavour were restricted to senior officers of peerage rank. Two Orders of Chivalry were available, the Order of the Thistle and the Order of the Garter. From time to time special commemorative medals were issued, but reserved for selected commanders only. With the revival of the Order of the Bath in 1725, military leaders who were not peers began to receive knighthoods as a reward for martial prowess. The institution of the Order of St Patrick in 1783 extended the award system to Ireland.

The expansion of empire from the mid-18th century resulted in Great Britain fighting campaigns in India, America, the West Indies and in the Mediterranean. Gradually there was an increase in the rank and number of individuals who received recognition but not in any official manner. It was left to trading companies and commanders to strike medals at their own expense for issue to officers and men.

The almost continuous warfare waged against Revolutionary France and the succeeding Napoleonic Empire from 1793 to 1815 can be regarded as the first total war undertaken by Great Britain. Initially the Royal Navy bore the brunt of the fighting and a Naval gold medal was struck by the Government in 1795 for officers of flag rank and captains. Army gold crosses and medals were authorized in 1811 with similar rank restrictions and it was not

A grenadier of the 25th Regiment of Foot, 1769.

until after the Battle of Waterloo in 1815 that a medal was struck for all participants in the battle, regardless of rank.

The issue of campaign medals really developed in the reign of Queen Victoria and since 1847 medals have been produced for most campaigns. As warfare became more complex, new decorations were instituted to fill the gap between campaign medals and Orders of Chivalry, so that bravery, distinguished leadership, or personal contribution could be recognized by an award. The best-known of these is the Victoria Cross, first granted in 1856. The Museum has ten VCs in the collection.

Military uniform

Scottish military uniform holds a unique position in the history of military costume. In a field where fashion and foreign influence have always been important, Scotland has developed one of the most famous national uniforms. Its history is explained through the uniform collections of the Scottish United Services Museum. This collection consists of uniforms worn by Scots in the three services from their formation to the present day, with special reference to the Scottish Regiments.

Scottish military uniform began with the formation of a professional Army in the late 17th century. The need for uniform dress for soldiers stemmed from the necessity for an army to identify both its friends and its enemies. Previously this had been done in different ways, from the wearing of coloured sashes to such simple devices as the placing of different leaves in men's hats. Uniform gave to the soldier an identity, whether in front of an enemy or an indifferent public. It could also communicate by its splendour the power and prestige of the state. Until modern times the Army and Royal Navy presented most people with a vision of strong government incarnate. Soldiers, ruled by harsh discipline and trained in rigid drill movements to behave as a synchronized mass, could not be allowed any expression of individuality, and especially not in their appearance.

Many items in the Museum's collection have few specifically Scottish features. Until the mid-18th century and the raising of the first Highland regiments the Scottish elements of the British Army were indistinguishable from any other. The Royal Navy and Royal Air Force, with occasional exceptions, have never indulged in national variations in their uniforms. In order to make the best use of the vast resource of manpower offered by the Highlands, the Army encouraged the wearing of a regimented version of the traditional Highland dress. When,

a generation later, the romantic revival of the Highlands was under way, the army provided the only continuous tradition of Highland dress. Consequently the newly created tartans and impedimenta inherited many features of military uniform.

The enthusiasm for tartan spread further in the services. All Scottish regiments, Highland or Lowland, now have some 'Highland' element to their uniform and character. Even the Scottish squadrons of the Royal Auxiliary Air Force of the 1930s insisted on having pipers in full Highland dress.

The Scottish United Services Museum traces these developments through numerous items of uniform, many of them unique and of international importance. The

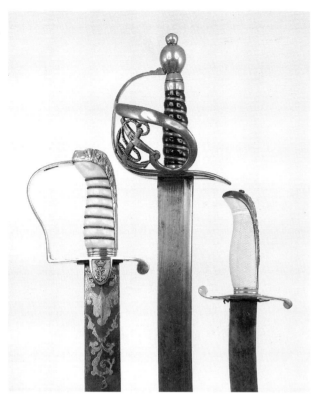

Hilts of three British naval edged
weapons, about 1780–1820.

bayonet as well as broadsword and dirk. The formalizing
and regulation of the British Army at the end of the 18th
century meant that items such as personal weapons were
categorized into standard patterns. Each of these frequently had a regimental sub-pattern, since such was
the nature of the Army, and the Museum's collections
reflect this wide variety of types and styles which continued
throughout the 19th and into the 20th century.

Naval weaponry is not neglected and, although sparse
in the types of firearm used aboard ship, the Museum's
collection is becoming stronger in the types of edged
weapon worn and used by sailors.

The collection of British military firearms is small
but becoming increasingly representative. Aside from the
Birmingham-made all-steel pistols issued to Highland soldiers until the American War of Independence, little
is uniquely Scottish since most types were carried by
most British soldiers. As the Scottish serviceman moves
into the technologically advanced final decade of the
20th century, it will become ever more necessary to
collect the types of modern firearm with which his role
is inextricably linked.

collection includes original 'sealed patterns' from the
Army Pattern Room of the 19th century, many of which
were unique experimental designs. Other important items
include the Seafield Collection: a massive array of equipment issued to a single regiment in the late 1790s. The
Museum also has a unique archive relating to the manufacture of uniforms. This includes the files of Wilson of
Bannockburn, the principal supplier of military tartan in
the 19th century and the sample and correspondence files
of William Anderson & Sons, for long the main Scottish
military outfitter.

Military weapons
see also Weaponry

The serviceman is characterized by his capacity to bear
and use arms and, as Scotland's national military museum,
the Scottish United Services Museum possesses an extensive array of most types of weapon carried by the
Scottish serviceman.

The bulk of the collection is centred upon late 18th- and
19th-century edged weapons, polearms and firearms. The
18th-century soldier used a formidable variety of personal
weapons and his Highland Scottish equivalent represented
a walking arsenal, equipped with pistols as well as musket,

Minerals
see also **Gems; Hydrocarbons; Semi-precious
stones**

Minerals are naturally occurring chemical compounds and
elements, usually of characteristic crystal form. The present National Museums of Scotland incorporate the older
Natural History Museum of the University of Edinburgh,
which contained many minerals collected before 1854 by
the Keeper, the mineralogist Professor Robert Jameson.
Although there may be many of these historic minerals in
the national collection, few can now be recognized.

The collections of Professor Matthew Forster Heddle
(1828–97) and Patrick Dudgeon form the nucleus of the
present collection. Dudgeon owned a yacht, and with
Heddle sailed along many stretches of Scottish coastline,
frequently landing to collect top-quality mineral specimens
from otherwise inaccessible localities. Heddle was professor of chemistry (1862–80) at St Andrews University
and a founder member, and second president (1879–81)
of the Mineralogical Society. His collection of about
7000 minerals and rocks came to the then Museum of
Science and Art in 1894 and Dudgeon's in 1890. With the
use of sophisticated instrumental techniques many
previously unsuspected minerals have been found in the
collections, including a new species named mattheddleite

Drum of the Strathspey Fencibles and
items associated with the 97th Regiment
of Foot, all from the Seafield Collection
of military antiquities, about 1795.
Military music: Military uniform

Breast star of a Knight of the Order
of the Thistle by Thomas Wirgman,
London, about 1815–20. **Military
orders, decorations and medals**

Far right doubly-terminated calcite crystal,
about 18 cms long, from Wanlockhead,
Dumfriesshire. **Minerals**

Part of the research collection of fishes.
Natural History Collections

Under Orders by Gemmell Hutchinson, RSA, 1882, showing soldiers of the Black Watch and their families in Edinburgh Castle before leaving for Egypt in July 1882. **Military art**

Late 17th-century gold pendants, one *left* with a cameo of Mary, Queen of Scots. **Medieval and Renaissance jewellery**

in 1987. Through bequests, donation and field collecting the collection of Scottish minerals has grown to its present size of about 15,000 specimens.

Minerals are most abundantly collected as a by-product of the economic exploitation of ore minerals. The national collection thus contains many different specimens of most of the 60 or so minerals recognized from the former world-famous lead-mining area of Leadhills, Wanlockhead in Lanarkshire and Dumfriesshire. The most noteworthy are lead–zinc minerals, exquisite calcite specimens, together with variegated hemimorphite (a zinc mineral) and pyromorphites. Several minerals have been named after the area, including Leadhillite, Lanarkite, Susannite (after the Susanna mine) and Caledonite (after Caledonia) which was first discovered in this area.

Scottish geology is diverse and well explored, so rock-forming minerals are well represented in the collection (see **Rocks**). Zeolites from Skye, and Mull lavas are rich in variety and form, rivalling those from Iceland. There is much interest in zeolites for their economic importance in industry, for example in water purification. Minerals formed due to heat and pressure, ores, innumerable varieties of silica, serpentine, carbonates and sulphates abound throughout the collection.

Of the approximately 3500 known mineral species, 480 have been recorded from Scotland; the national collection contains almost 300 of them.

Modern science

Age alone frequently provides sufficient reason for veneration. The passage of time certainly allows judgements to be less influenced by contemporary 'hype', but as Victorian curators well knew, the past began yesterday.

Collecting material related to the practice of science in the decades since 1920 is constrained by a number of factors including the sheer proliferation of material, the increasing rate of innovation and greater subject specialism. The first factor means that collecting must be selective, the second that considered appraisal of significance is difficult, and the third that external expertise must often be sought. A fourth factor is scale. With the exception of a handful of massive observatory instruments, most pre-20th-century scientific instruments are relatively small. Some modern laboratory apparatus is also small, indeed miniaturization has been one of the technical achievements of the last two decades. However, much pioneering work required either a massive installation of equipment, or an assemblage of material.

To allow collecting to be guided only by what can be readily handled would warp the historical record. The attempt to provide, through collecting, a balanced record for the future is governed by selectivity and pragmatism. There is a wealth of objects that might be collected to create a material record of scientific endeavour in recent decades. The selection is biased towards objects in the physical sciences with a Scottish provenance. A few examples will indicate the flavour of present judgements.

From the University of Edinburgh is the one million volt Cockcroft-Walton linear accelerator, made by Philips of Eindhoven and used for 20 years from the early 1950s for research in nuclear physics. This piece of apparatus is some eight metres high, including the control room, but even to the uninitiated it is an impressive sight.

Hidden behind its bland fascia panels, the electronic computer of the 1980s has little obvious appeal, and there are problems in explaining how such machines work and the significance of particular innovations, whilst retaining general public interest. But the Ferranti Argus 500 computer in the collections had a vital role – until 1987 it monitored and controlled the flow of oil from BP's North Sea wells to the refinery at Grangemouth.

Smaller in size, but with technology no less hard to present, is a group of infra-red and ultra-violet spectrometers, used routinely in laboratory analysis from the 1950s until the present day. Drawing on the advice of current practitioners, the Museums have attempted to collect a representative sample from research laboratories in industry and the universities.

Contemporary photograph of apparatus used in pioneering the spectrographic analysis of soils at the Macaulay Institute for Soil Research, Aberdeen, about 1936. (*The Macaulay Institute*)

In the Insect Study Room, working on part of the vast entomological collection.

Taxidermist preparing a wild-cat for display.

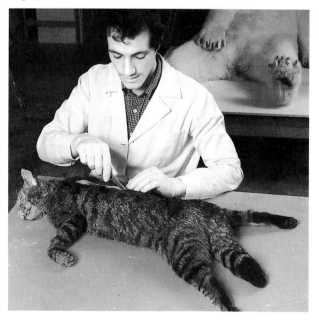

Music
see Bagpipes; Harps; Military music

Navigation
see Astronomy, navigation and surveying

Natural History Collections

The natural history collections comprise well over two million zoological specimens, ranging from elephants and whales to insects, worms and microscopic animals. The material comes from every part of the world including the oceans and polar regions.

The history of the collections can be traced back to the mid-17th century. Natural history specimens were among the first to be exhibited when the present Chambers Street building opened in 1866. In the early years of the Museum virtually all material was put on display but modern museum practice now treats specimens intended for display and those intended for research in different ways. Display specimens are mounted or cast in life-like poses. A wide selection of animals from all over the world, including many from Scotland, is exhibited in the Chambers Street building. The Scottish material on display provides an important educational resource, helping towards an understanding of the Scottish environment and wildlife. However, it is the research material, preserved behind the scenes, that makes up by far the largest part of the natural history collections. This research aspect generally goes unnoticed by the general public.

The natural history research collections are among the largest in the British Isles and are of international importance. Along with other major museum collections, they play an important role in taxonomic research, the process by which species are described and classified. Animals are very variable, and large numbers of specimens need to be examined from as wide a geographic area as possible. This is why natural history collections usually contain many examples of each species. The National Museums, with their unrivalled holdings of Scottish material and large collections from further afield, are consulted by scientists, natural historians and other specialists from all over the world. As taxonomic research depends on many sources of material the Museums are an integral strand in a giant web of international co-operation.

The collections also have an important local role as a focus for natural history research in Scotland. They serve as reference collections for identification, providing the large series of accurately identified specimens against which specimens of unknown identity can be compared.

The collections are also a repository for 'voucher' specimens which provide the evidence to support published distribution or biological records. Such specimens deposited in the collections remain available for future examination if their identification should ever come into question.

Animals do not respect political borders and so it is generally not useful to study the animals of one country in isolation from those of neighbouring regions. For this reason the National Museums, although rich in Scottish specimens, have no separate Scottish natural history collections, and Scottish specimens are kept together with other material where they are of most general use.

Oceanography
see also **History of physical science**

Funded jointly by the Admiralty and the Royal Society of London, the 1872–76 scientific expedition of HMS *Challenger* was led by the professor of natural history in the University of Edinburgh, C W Wyville Thomson. The chemist on the expedition was another Scot, J Y Buchanan.

The collections include apparatus used and designed by Buchanan, such as mid-water sampling bottles and thermometer reversing frames. The Scottish contribution to the Challenger expedition helped to motivate the Scottish National Antarctic Expedition (1902–4), led by W S Bruce. There is apparatus used on board *Scotia* on this expedition, and more from the Scottish Oceanographic Laboratory founded in 1907.

Optics
see also **History of physical science**

The earliest Scottish made microscope in the collections is dated 1743 and was made by John Finlayson, mathematical instrument-maker in Edinburgh. The mechanical design, whilst pleasing to the eye, is technically naïve. During the 1745 uprising Finlayson served as an engineer in the Jacobite army. He subsequently drew and engraved a map of the battlefield of Culloden – and was rewarded for his pains by imprisonment.

There are a number of examples of the kaleidoscope – the optical toy patented in 1818 by David Brewster (1781–1868). Almost overnight the instrument achieved amazing success, with literally hundreds of thousands being made and sold in Paris and London. Unable to enforce the patent, Brewster did not make a fortune and

The Scottish Oceanographic Laboratory showing material from the Scottish National Antarctic expedition, much of which came to the Museum in 1921.

Prism cut from Iceland spar, showing
its double refraction property.

The Edinburgh Pewterers' touchplate,
stamped with the marks, or touches, of
Edinburgh pewterers from about 1590
to about 1750.

had to be content with being a leading figure in 19th-century scientific endeavour in Scotland.

It was at Brewster's instigation that the Royal Society of Edinburgh commissioned Alexander Adie to make the impressive prototype polarizing microscope now preserved in the Museums. Though technically interesting, this instrument was almost immediately superseded following the demonstration of the double refracting properties of a prism cut from Iceland spar by William Nicol, a private teacher of natural philosophy in Edinburgh. A small nicol prism, made by the inventor himself, was presented to the Industrial Museum of Scotland in 1856 (see *page 9*), and is still in the collections.

Paintings
see **Man and beast; Military art**

Paper making
see **Textile, paper and printing industries**

Pewter

Pewter, a mixture of tin and lead, has been used in Scotland since Roman times, but it is not until the 15th century that there are records of craftsmen actually making pewter vessels.

Pewterers were members of the Hammermen's Incorporations (see **Domestic silver**), and the master of the Pewterers was empowered to test the quality of the metal and destroy anything that was not up to standard (in general, the higher the percentage of tin in pewter, the better the quality). The Edinburgh Pewterers' Touch Plates were the physical guarantee that those pewterers who stamped their marks on them were binding themselves to use only the approved quality of metal. These plates, now in the National Museums along with the Pewterers' Common Box, were also a record of each craftsman's 'touch', or trademark, which he stamped on his completed wares. They have the touches of 129 pewterers, dating from about 1590 to 1760.

Pewter was used for making most kinds of domestic and church vessels, being cheaper than silver and more durable than wood. Early Scottish pewter is rare, however, as it deteriorates rapidly with age if not properly cared for. One of the earliest pieces in the Museums is a fine rosewater dish by Richard Weir of Edinburgh. Made sometime between 1603 and 1625, it has a central enamelled boss with the arms of King James VI and I.

The collections contain many later examples. One of the commonest uses of pewter was for tavern and public house measures and drinking vessels. The best-known type of Scottish measure was the 'tappit hen'. It is similar in shape to the cider flagons of Normandy and its name may well be French in origin. The largest tappit hen – the Scots pint, equivalent to three imperial pints – would not have been drunk from directly, but used to fill a smaller cup or quaich (see **Quaichs**).

Other types of pewter measure were also used, including the baluster, which was common in Scotland and England from the 16th century. Pear-shaped and pot-bellied vessels were also popular in Scotland, with variations in style being associated with pewterers in Edinburgh, Glasgow and Aberdeen.

The use of pewter for domestic vessels began to decline with the increasing popularity of other, cheaper and more convenient materials such as pottery, glass and electro-plated silver.

Photographs
see **Military art; Photography; Scottish Ethnological Archive**

Photography
see also **History of physical science**

A large collection of apparatus used by the photographic pioneer W H F Talbot is preserved in the National Museums. Though Talbot had extensive correspondence with the Scottish optical scientist David Brewster, himself a notable early photographic experimenter, none of this material has any Scottish provenance. There is, however, an early daguerreotype camera, unsigned but attributable to Thomas Davidson, and made in Edinburgh in the early 1840s. Two volumes of calotype photographs taken by Dr John Adamson, Robert Adamson and D O Hill have some of the earliest calotypes taken in Scotland, including what John Adamson maintained was the first Scottish portrait photograph. Hill and Robert Adamson were amongst the most energetic pioneers in photography.

Pictish symbols

The Picts first appear in historical texts in the 3rd century AD as the people living in eastern Scotland beyond the Forth, beyond, that is, the Roman Empire. Yet it was several centuries before their most distinctive creation,

'Tappit hen', *left* possibly made by William Hunter, Edinburgh, 18th century.

Daguerrotype camera, unsigned, but probably made by Thomas Davidson, Edinburgh, after 1840.

Some of the massive Pictish silver chains found in eastern Scotland.

large undressed stones decorated with a variety of symbols, made their appearance in the Scottish landscape. Over time and under the impulse of Christian belief and associated manuscripts, these stones became elaborate cross-slabs (see **Early Christianity**) although it was a long time before the earlier symbols totally disappeared. Even though many of the finest stones remain part of the Scottish countryside the national collections contain an impressive range of this sculpture including the outstanding stone from Hilton of Cadboll, Ross and Cromarty.

There are essentially three groups of symbols: animals, birds or fishes; those that can plausibly be interpreted as objects; and decorative devices. Many of the animal symbols are readily recognizable, such as the bull from East Lomond Hill, Fife, the deer from Grantown, Moray, and the goose and fish from Easterton of Roseisle, Moray. Others, however, are clearly imaginary. Similarly, some of the object symbols such as mirrors and combs are easily identified while others are more problematic. The final group of symbols involves apparently abstract designs which defy interpretation. There is a substantial degree of patterning in the combination of symbols that appear on individual stones and this has led to a number of attempts to interpret the symbols. None of these has met with widespread acceptance.

Although these symbols occur most commonly on large stones apparently erected specifically for display they also occur on the walls of caves, as at Covesea, Moray, and Wemyss, Fife, and on a small number of portable objects. Most of the latter are in the National Museums. Quite the most spectacular of these are the massive silver chains, two of which from Whitecleuch, Lanarkshire, and Parkhill, Aberdeenshire, have their terminal rings decorated with symbols. Other silver objects from Norrie's Law, Fife, similarly decorated, are two identical plaques and a large hand-pin. In this case, as perhaps also with the silver chains, the symbols are inlaid with red enamel. A more mundane use of symbols may be seen on, for example, an ox phalangeal bone from the Broch of Burrian, North Ronaldsay, Orkney.

Plants: fossil

With over 5000 specimens and an extensive microscope slide collection, fossil plants in the National Museums span the geological periods from the later Precambrian, 700 million years ago (Ma), to the Tertiary (40 Ma). Calcareous marine algae were important as rock builders from the time of the oldest rocks on earth (about 3500 Ma) through to Palaeozoic times (600–250 Ma). They are known from the Dalradian (700 Ma) of the western Highlands.

The oldest British fossils known are plants: algal spores from the Torridonian (1800 Ma) of Wester Ross. Filament-like algae resembling modern forms first appear in Ordovician rocks (500 Ma) and these are represented in the national collections by material from Girvan, and by Silurian (430 Ma) forms from the Pentland Hills (see **Fossils**). Among these algae were the probable ancestors of the first vascular land plants – those with a system for conducting water throughout the plant. Some of these plants occur in the Old Red Sandstone (405 Ma) of Angus, and the collections contain the type specimens (see **Fossils**) of a species of *Cooksonia*, the earliest genus of land plants, and of the earliest *Zosterophyllum*, a member of the group ancestral to today's clubmosses. These earliest land plants were small, simple, shoot-like plants, reproducing by means of spores. Our most complete knowledge of them comes from specimens exquisitely preserved in a silicified Devonian (400 Ma) peat bog at Rhynie, Aberdeenshire.

Silver plaques engraved with symbols, originally filled with red enamel, from Norrie's Law, Fife, 7th century AD.

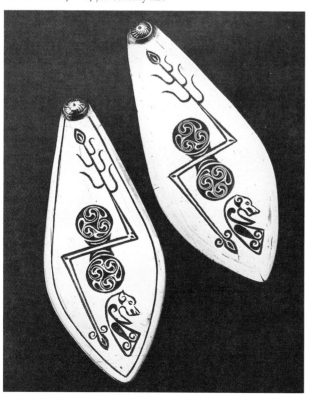

Such spore-bearing plants, needing wet places to re-produce, are incompletely adapted for life on land. Land plants totally liberated from the water only occurred with the evolution of the seed, the earliest known being Devonian (365 Ma). Albert Long's discoveries of Car-boniferous (350 Ma) seeds in Berwickshire are among palaeobotany's most important advances this century. In Long's collections in the Museums are about 2000 micro-scope slides, revealing some of the earliest stages in the evolution of seeds.

Scotland is unusual in yielding well-preserved, early Carboniferous (345 Ma) plants. Some of these came from a now inaccessible limestone at Burdiehouse, Edinburgh. Specimens in the Museums' Hugh Miller Collection (see **Fishes: fossil**) figure in his *Testimony of the Rocks* (1857), whilst others were illustrated in Lindley and Hutton's *Fossil flora of Great Britain* (1831–3).

Although there is as yet no completely reconstructed Lower Carboniferous plant, new plants continue to be discovered, most recently from the Museums' excavation at Bathgate (see **Amphibians: fossil**). The later Carboni-ferous (300 Ma) is characterized by coal-swamp plants: shrubby seed-ferns and tree-sized clubmosses and horse-tails. These are well represented in the Robert Dunlop Collection, which contains specimens illustrated in Robert Kidston's monumental *Fossil plants of the Carboniferous rocks of Great Britain* (1923–76).

Seed-plants, especially conifers, have exceeded spore-bearers since the Mesozoic (250 Ma). One formerly abundant group of seed plants, the cycads or tropical tree-ferns, just survives today. The Hugh Miller Col-lection contains the first recognized (1857) fossil cycads from Scotland, in Jurassic rocks (160 Ma) of Helmsdale, Sutherland. Leaves from the Tertiary (40 Ma) of the Inner Hebrides represent familiar warm to temperate trees and other flowering plants which have dominated the earth since their origin, about 130 million years ago.

Post-Reformation church furnishings
see also **Pre-Reformation church furnishings and relics**

After the Reformation of 1560 two main factors seem to have determined the provision and furnishing of churches; the initial poverty of the new church and its reformed doctrine.

Its poverty, caused by the diversion of much of the old church's wealth into secular hands, meant that many churches were sparsely furnished, with little or no fixed

Cone of one of the first recognized specimens of fossil cycad (tropical tree fern, Jurassic, 160 million years ago) from Scotland, as illustrated by Hugh Miller, 1857.

furniture. It could be argued that the disappearance of many of the Catholic Church's treasures owes more to the rapacity of the secular lords who controlled many of the churches before the Reformation than to the iconoclasm of the Reformers.

Emphasis was on the preaching of the Gospel and there-fore the pulpit was a major element in the church. Very few early pulpits survive. The National Museums have two fascinating examples: a fairly ornately carved pulpit from Parton in Kirkcudbrightshire, and the pulpit which is said to have been used by John Knox when he preached at St Giles. Whether or not it was used by the father of the Scottish Reformation, which seems unlikely, it is a good example of the type of woodwork in a late 16th- or early 17th-century Scottish church.

Another famous relic of church history is the small folding stool known as 'Jenny Geddes' stool'. Again it seems unlikely that she ever launched it at Knox's head, but it is important evidence of the type of furniture used in a late 17th-century kirk. There seem to have been very few fixed pews for the common people, these being reserved mainly for the 'Laird's Loft' or the Merchants and Trades Incorporations in the burgh kirks.

The Reformed Kirk had only two sacraments: Com-munion and Baptism, and Kirk leaders were concerned that churches should provide themselves with appropriate vessels. An Act of 1617 stated that all parish kirks were to have 'Basines and Lavoiris for...Baptism, and couppes, tablis and table clothe, for...holie Communion'. There

Silver communion cups and bread plate,
and baptismal basin and ewer, 17th
century.

are earlier communion cups in existence, such as the one from Rosneath, made by James Mossman of Edinburgh in 1585, but this Act led to an upsurge in the production of silver church plate. One of the most prolific makers was Gilbert Kirkwood in Edinburgh who made many beautiful and elegant cups, such as those he made for Balmaghie in 1617–19.

Much early 17th-century church silver shows that the Kirk did not totally despise decoration or beauty, although it did not view them as sacred in themselves. When commissioning a pair of cups from the Canongate goldsmith George Ziegler, the session of Bolton Kirk decreed that if the money were ever needed for the care of the poor, the cups were to be melted down again.

The Act of 1617 did not specify the material which the vessels were to be made from – there was no doctrinal insistence on silver – and many kirks, particularly the poorer ones, supplied themselves with cheaper pewter vessels (see **Pewter**). The earliest surviving

examples in the Museums are the beakers and breadplate from Keig in Aberdeenshire. Also of pewter, or lead, and an integral part of Communion, were the tokens which admitted parishioners to the Sacrament. These were given out by the elders to those who had proved they were worthy to take Communion. Every kirk in Scotland had these communion tokens, the equivalent of the modern communion card, and the Museums have a definitive collection of them.

The elders' role in communion is one example of ecclesiastical discipline, but there were many others, for the Kirk played a vital part in the exercise of social control. Their discipline may seem harsh and repressive by today's standards, and indeed has been blamed for much of Scotland's collective neurosis, but it should be remembered that the Kirk was often the only agency able to perform a policing function. Objects connected with this role are another aspect of material associated with the Post-Reformation Church (see **Instruments of punishment and torture**).

Post-Roman weights and measures
see also **Weights and measures**

The discovery of exotic objects presents considerable difficulties for archaeologists. Even supposing that there had been no movement of the people for whom these objects were a part of material culture, a number of possible explanations for their presence remain, such as loot, trade or gift-exchange. Thus, although trade between groups may be a normal feature of life in a particular area and the resulting objects become part of the archaeological record, it does not follow that this is clearly recognized by archaeologists.

What does help is the recovery of items that are an integral part of trade. The most obvious example is standardized coinage. But Scotland in the second half of the first millennium AD was essentially coin-less and we must, therefore, look for other indicative objects. This is by no means straightforward as merchants use few tools that are unique to them.

Balance beam and two pans with a set of weights, from a Viking grave at Kiloran Bay, Colonsay, 9th–10th century.

One group of items that might fit this requirement is weights and measures. Certainly, the need to weigh is not exclusive to merchants but where the devices seem concerned with small quantities of valuable commodities the interpretation may have some credibility. Finds of this kind are not numerous, although relatively well represented in the Museums' collections.

The Viking silver hoards (see **Viking silver hoards**) and other earlier finds suggest that silver bullion was in use in place of coins. Where coins occur they are always imports, mainly from the Anglo-Saxon or Arabic worlds, and are treated as bullion. Clearly then, weight is an important, though not exclusive, means of measuring payment.

The most important Scottish find is the pair of scales and set of seven lead weights with ornamental mounts found in a Norse burial at Kiloran Bay, Colonsay. Interestingly, two of these weights are decorated with insular enamel work showing motifs that are clearly derived from Arabic script. Whether the prototypes arrived from contacts with Moorish North Africa and Spain or by way of Russia and Scandinavia cannot be determined. Two non-Viking hoards of the 9th century contain items of weighing equipment: part of a balance beam from Croy, Inverness-shire, and an elaborately decorated weight from Talnotrie, Kirkcudbrightshire.

Pottery: factory-made
see also **Pottery: hand-made**

Industrial production of pottery in Scotland began in the mid-18th century, although it is clear that there was a well-developed pre-industrial pottery industry from at least the 17th century.

From the mid-18th century mass-produced wares, made by techniques developed in the Industrial Revolution, can be attributed (however tentatively) to individual factories. In this early period, however, documentation is scarce. Many potteries were making similar wares and potters themselves travelled around, taking techniques and patterns with them. Even sherd evidence from unknown sites must be interpreted cautiously and new work is changing old received ideas about identification.

By the second half of the 18th century there were potteries in Glasgow and around the Firth of Forth. Delftfield in Glasgow is one of the first to have reasonable documentation. It was established in 1748 and was soon producing delftware, that is tin-glazed earthenware, and later creamware and pearlware. The National

Punchbowl with transfer-printed scene of
'Port Hopetoun', Edinburgh by Watson's
Pottery, Prestonpans, early 19th century.

Museums have two delftware soup plates from a service for the Murray of Polmaise family.

Potteries had also been established on the south shore of the Forth. A pair of porcelain mugs, with the crest of the Dalrymples of Overhailes, in the Museums, are from William Littler's pottery at West Pans, near Edinburgh. By the early 1800s potteries in Musselburgh, Portobello and Prestonpans, all near Edinburgh, were producing a wide range of wares, from soft-paste porcelain, such as the Musselburgh Arms jug of 1822 by William Reid, to transfer-printed earthenware, like the punchbowl showing Port Hopetoun, Edinburgh, by Watson's of Prestonpans.

Throughout the 19th century the number of potteries grew, to meet the increased demand from the growing mass market. Many areas supported their own concerns, but the largest firms were centred on the Forth and Clyde rivers. Kirkcaldy became a major centre, with four main firms, including Robert Heron and Co, famous for

'Overhailes' mug, late 18th century,
'Musselburgh Arms' jug, 1822 and a soup
plate from the Murray of Polmaise
service, late 18th century.

their prestigious Wemyss ware. The collection has a representative selection of this highly decorative ware.

Glasgow, however, had the greatest number of factories, the most important of which seems to have been the firm of J & M P Bell & Co. The firm began about 1842 and was soon making a wide range of high-quality goods. Like many other potteries in the second half of the 19th century, however, their most popular ware was transfer-printed earthenware, which was durable, decorative and affordable by the masses. Some designs were extremely well produced.

Bells, like other firms, had a large export trade, and the height of their commercial achievement was the production of a startling series of oriental patterns exclusively for South-east Asia. The Museums have a comprehensive collection of over 200 plates from this eastern trade, showing patterns in up to eight different colour schemes.

Most Scottish potteries did not adapt well to the changed economic climate of the 20th century, and those that survived the First World War soon declined, giving way to small-scale art potteries and individual craftsmen.

Pottery: hand-made
see also Pottery: factory-made

From the 12th century skilled professional potters began to establish themselves in Scotland. The National Museums have a collection of several thousand medieval and later sherds and complete vessels from all over Scotland including kiln material from Colstoun, East Lothian and Throsk, near Stirling and collections from Bothwell Castle, Lanarkshire, Glenluce Abbey, Wigtownshire and Kelso Abbey, Roxburghshire. There are also several hundred floor tiles from North Berwick, Newbattle Abbey, Midlothian, and elsewhere. The collection represents the major aspects and developments of pottery in Scotland.

Before the 12th century the Scots had got by with little or no pottery and such as they had was normally crudely made. The pottery now produced extensively was earthenware, turned on a wheel, and often covered with a lead glaze giving a green, yellow or brown finish to the vessels. The potters made a wide variety of wares including lamps, distilling equipment, and ewers in the form of animals (aquamaniles) but their standard products were jugs, storage jars and cooking pots. Some, however, specialized in producing floor tiles for monastic churches and the houses of the rich. The remains of such a kiln producing finely decorated tiles have been discovered in the grounds of a convent at North Berwick where it was set up in the 13th century.

Most kilns were in the countryside next to clay deposits and within easy reach of their main markets. Kilns at Colstoun in East Lothian in the 13th and 14th centuries supplied Haddington and the surrounding area, and other kilns are known to have served centres such as Aberdeen,

'Pirlie pigs', two *left* 16th century and
one 19th century.

Perth and the Tweed Valley. The pots sold very cheaply and were used by all classes in towns and burghs and throughout most of the Lowlands.

It was only in the 17th century that the use of pottery spread to all parts of the country. Much of the production was now in the hands of part-time potters/farmers. Their pots were poorly made and clumsy in appearance. A well documented group was working at Throsk. Some called themselves piggers from 'pig', the old Scots word for an earthenware vessel, and one of their most distinctive products, little money boxes, are known as pirlie pigs.

Much pottery was also traded into Scotland from England and the Continent, often as containers for other commodities. From the 14th century German stoneware jugs and flagons were brought in in large quantities and from the 16th century delftware with a smooth white fabric, painted and covered with a tin glaze. In the Western Isles a native tradition of building pots, known as croggans, by hand, survived into the 20th century. Of particular interest is Barvas ware, made in Lewis in imitation of factory-produced teasets.

Power for industry

Until the development of a widespread public electricity supply, industry had to provide its own power. Each factory needed an engine of some sort to drive its machinery. In the 19th and early 20th century this was most commonly a steam engine, but at various times water wheels and turbines, or gas and oil engines were used as alternatives.

It is not surprising therefore that from the foundation of the Industrial Museum of Scotland in 1854 (see *page 9*) power for industry was one of the major topics covered. The collection, both of models and full-size engines, is large and most of the major technical developments are illustrated. To begin with, the objects in the collection were mainly small full-size machines, or models, but during the last 20 years, as the survivors of the pre-electrical age came to the end of their working lives, a few large full-size examples have been acquired.

The oldest engine in the collection is a Newcomen-type steam engine built at Carron Ironworks, near Falkirk, about 1780. This is a very important specimen, an example of the first practical form of steam engine, which was introduced in the English Midlands in 1712. Where the engine worked first is unknown, but in 1806 it was moved to Caprington Colliery, near Kilmarnock. There it worked until 1901, pumping water from the pit.

Boulton and Watt steam engine of 1786, which worked at the Barclay Perkins brewery, London.

James Watt made two major changes in the design of Newcomen's steam engine. The first, patented in 1769, was the use of a separate condenser. In a Newcomen engine the steam was condensed by a spray of cold water into the working cylinder itself. This cold spray also cooled the metal of the cylinder, which had to be reheated by the incoming steam during each working stroke of the engine. Watt's second development was the 'rotative' engine, in other words an engine capable of driving any type of machinery.

The Newcomen engine and the early Watt engines could only be used to raise and lower the plunger of a pump and their use was therefore almost entirely restricted to the drainage of mine workings.

The separate condenser dramatically reduced fuel consumption and the development of the rotative engine greatly increased the uses of steam power. Both features are illustrated by the Museums' Boulton & Watt engine of

Waterwheel, 1826, at Woodside Mill, near
Aberdeen, before being dismantled and
moved to the Royal Scottish Museum in
1967. *(SDD, Historic Buildings and
Monuments Division)*

1786 which worked at the London brewery of Barclay
Perkins & Co for almost 100 years.

When large-scale industrialization started in the last
quarter of the 18th century with the mechanization of
cotton spinning, sufficiently powerful steam engines were
not available. The early spinning mills such as those
at New Lanark and Stanley, near Perth, therefore used
large water wheels. Such water wheels were occasionally installed in preference to steam power in the early
19th century, where conditions were particularly suitable. A 25 ft (7.6 m) wheel of 150 hp, built in 1826 by the
Manchester firm of Hewes and Wren, remained at work
in Aberdeenshire until 1965. It is now on display in the
Royal Museum of Scotland, Chambers Street.

The collection of steam engine models, small full-size
engines and engine details illustrates the great diversity of
19th-century steam technology. A particularly notable
engine is a beam engine built in 1826 which worked
at a brewery in Margate until 1950. Engines built in
the 18th century had substantial quantities of wood in
their construction, but this example shows the later all-
iron construction. The maker is unknown, but it was
built originally for export as part of a consignment of
sugar machinery. The ship was wrecked near the North
Foreland but the engine was salvaged. In the 1820s
Glasgow was a very important centre for the manufacture
of sugar machinery and it is possible that the engine was
made there.

The collection includes other small beam engines showing different forms of construction and examples of the various designs of vertical and horizontal engines which superseded the beam engine. Most were made and almost all were used in Scotland.

Steam technology was an international matter and from the mid-19th century major contributions were being made by American and Continental firms. Their work became widely diffused and the collection has major specimens illustrating this process.

In 1849 the American engineer George H Corliss developed a distinctive form of valve-operating mechanism which greatly improved speed regulation and was claimed to reduce steam consumption. This Corliss valve gear became almost universal for large factory engines built in Britain, and it was also very popular in some Continental countries. The earliest British builder of these engines was Robert Douglas (later Douglas & Grant) of Kirkcaldy who produced his first in 1863 for a paper mill on the Water of Leith. In 1876 the Museum Workshop completed a model of a Douglas & Grant Corliss engine, using drawings lent by the firm. Then in 1979 a full-size engine, built in 1923 and one of the last produced by Douglas & Grant, was acquired from a woollen mill in Alva.

Another distinctive form of valve mechanism was that developed in Switzerland by Sulzer Brothers in 1865. This became widely used, particularly in Germany, and was also taken up by a number of British engine builders including several in Scotland. Probably the largest steam engine in the collection is the Sulzer-style machine of about 350 hp, built in 1923 by James Carmichael & Co of Dundee. This powered a large sawmill in Leven and was acquired in 1981.

Lacking the technical sophistication of the Sulzer and Corliss engines is a large but simple and rugged engine, with vacuum pump, built by the Harvey Engineering Company, Glasgow, in 1919 for a London sugar refinery. It came to the Museum in 1981.

Towards the end of the 19th century a new market for steam engines was developing as the electricity supply industry became established. Because generators operated at a high speed, special engine designs were evolved and in due course the steam turbine was developed. Notable among the high-speed engines was a fully enclosed design built by Willans and Robinson, in Surrey. The collection includes an example of this type, complete with its generator. It dates from about 1890 and was used in the Dundee area.

The leading name in steam turbine development in Britain was Charles Parsons. The Museums have an early example of a Parsons turbine and generator of 1890, used to provide electric lighting on a warship. Among the Continental designs represented in the collection by a model is the early 20th-century Zoelly turbine which originated in Germany but was also manufactured in Glasgow, under licence, by James Howden & Co.

Steam engines are of no practical use without boilers and the collection includes many boiler models as well as fullsize examples of the various fittings such as models as well as full-size examples of the various fittings such as valves and gauges essential for safe operation. There are also a number of full-size boilers. One of the oldest surviving boilers anywhere in Britain is an early 19th-century waggon boiler (so called because of its shape) which was found at a farm near Forfar in 1986. A leading Glasgow boiler-maker was the firm of Penman & Co and its work is represented by a small Cornish boiler of 1922 which worked at Millport Gasworks. The Cornish boiler originated, as the name suggests, in Cornwall, but quickly became one of the standard types of industrial boiler, made and used throughout Britain. Popular with small-scale users of steam, because of the low initial cost, was the vertical cross-tube boiler. An example of this type forms part of the plant at Biggar Gasworks. It is maintained in working order by the Museums.

Small-scale power users much preferred to dispense with a boiler altogether, and when gas engines, and later oil engines, became available in the latter part of the 19th century they gained widespread acceptance. Unfortunately few manufacturers of these engines became established in Scotland and most of the numerous examples in the collection, while used in Scotland, were manufactured elsewhere. However, there is a gas engine by Pollock, Whyte & Waddel of Johnstone and oil engines by Allan Brothers of Aberdeen, Alexander Shanks & Son, Arbroath, and the Atlantic Engine Co, Wishaw.

Two of the non-Scottish engines are of special importance, simply because preserved examples of such large engines are very rare.

A three-cylinder vertical gas engine of 120 hp, built in 1925 by the National Gas Engine Company, Ashton-under-Lyne, was acquired from Granton Gasworks, Edinburgh. The collection also includes one of the oldest Diesel oil engines in existence anywhere in the world. It was built in 1901 by the original German builder of such engines, M.A.N. of Augsburg, for a waterworks in Derbyshire. Similar engines were also built in Scotland by the first

Carved wooden figure of St Andrew from Fife, about 1500: it probably formed part of an altar retable.

The Fetternear banner, about 1520: detail.

Medieval and later earthenware vessels, including a croggan and two 'pirlie pigs'.
Pottery: hand-made

British company licensed to use Diesel's patents, The Mirrlees Watson Company, Glasgow.

Pre-Reformation church furnishings and relics
see also **Post-Reformation church furnishings**

The presence and power of the Church in medieval Scotland was extensive. Many buildings and institutions came within its control, cathedrals, monasteries and collegiate churches as well as parish churches. It was often able to harness the best available skills in the production of rich furnishings and fine decoration.

Much of this material has not survived – church buildings were often the targets of violence – but the National Museums nevertheless have an important collection. It includes individual items of great distinction and symbolic significance as well as material related to ordinary worship.

Stone and wood carving were a common form of decoration. A 13th-century sandstone altar top from Coldingham Priory, Berwickshire and part of a 15th-century altarpiece found in Edinburgh are examples. There is also fine stone carving from the Highlands, including a font, 1530, from the Church of St Maelrubha in Skye, and several burial monuments carved by local sculptors. The most notable wood carving is the figure of St Andrew from Fife, about 1500, which probably also came from an altarpiece. The collections contain two 15th-century carved choir stalls from Lincluden Collegiate Church near Dumfries.

Textiles also had their place amongst church furnishings. The Museums have a red velvet frontal, a covering for the altar front, which may have belonged to Mary, Queen of Scots. The Fetternear Banner, 1520, is the oldest known surviving example of Scottish embroidery (see **Embroidery**). It was probably an altar curtain in St Giles Cathedral, Edinburgh.

The utensils used in the Mass were often richly decorated. There are two silver chalices and pattens from Whithorn Priory, Wigtownshire found in 14th-century graves. Also from Whithorn is a gilt and enamelled crosier head, English work of the late 12th century. Dating from the 13th century are a bronze censer from the old church at Garvock, Kincardineshire, a figure of Christ found in a churchyard at Ceres, Fife and a candlestick from Kinnoull Parish Church, Perthshire. The latter are examples of the copper enamelled material that was being imported from Limoges, France at that time.

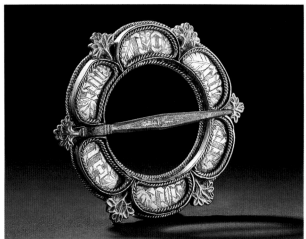

Delftware, porcelain and earthenware, late 18th and early 19th centuries. **Pottery: factory-made**

Silver-gilt brooch of about 1500 from Kindrochit Castle, Braemar, Aberdeenshire. **Ring brooches**

Earthenware floor tiles from the nunnery at North Berwick, 13th century. **Pre-Reformation church furnishings and relics**

Interior of the retort house at Biggar Gasworks Museum. **Public utilities**

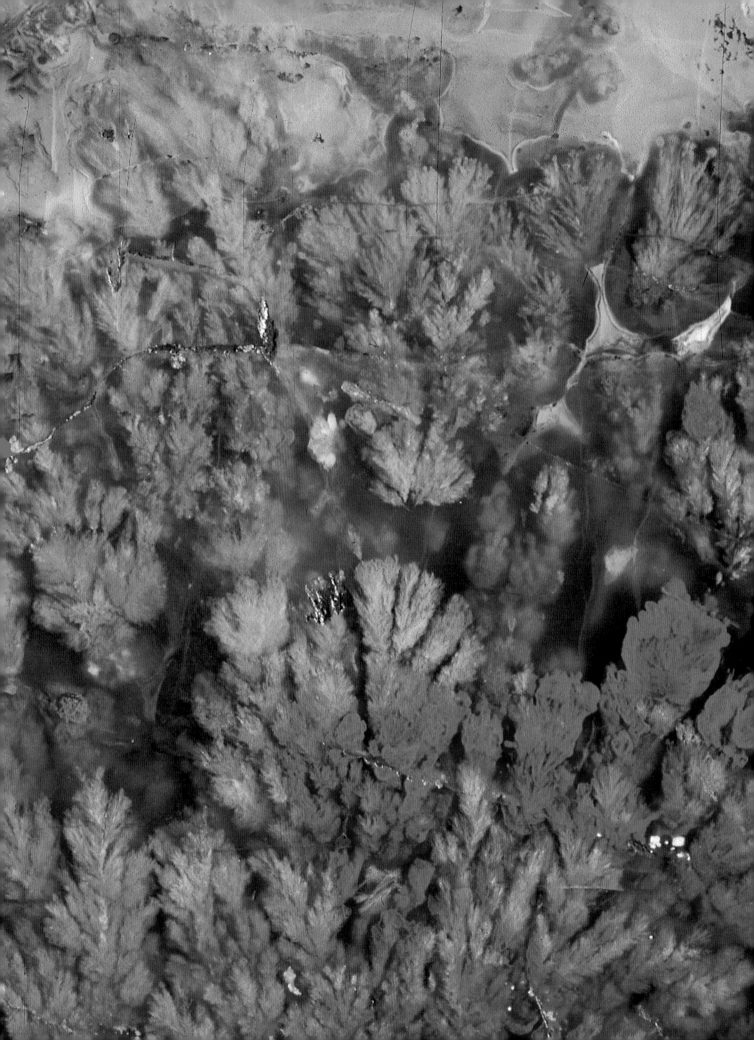

Slice of fine moss agate with natural iron staining, from Broughty Ferry, Angus: from the Miln Collection. **Semiprecious stones**

The relics of saints have a special significance. The Museums have two bell shrines, containers for small bells. From Kilmichael Glassary, Argyll is a 12th-century bronze example, holding an iron bell. The second is of West Highland origin although it was kept for a long time at Guthrie Castle, Angus. Its silver and bronze decoration was applied successively from the 12th to the 16th century.

Some relics have been in the care of hereditary keepers and this has ensured their survival. Connected with St Fillan are a 15th-century bell and crosier shrine, known as the *Coicrich*. The crosier went to Canada in 1818 with its hereditary keeper, where it was found and purchased by Professor Daniel Wilson, and returned to Edinburgh. The Monymusk reliquary, a portable house shrine of about AD 750 linked with the early spread of Christianity in Scotland (see **Early Christianity**), has particularly evocative associations. It was believed to be the Brecbennoch of St Columba, a talisman carried before the Scottish army in battle. St Fillan's crosier has a similar significance: it is said to have been with Robert the Bruce on the eve of the battle of Bannockburn.

Printing
see **Textile, paper and printing industries**

Prints
see **Military art**

Pseudo-penannular brooches

Pseudo-penannular brooches are so-called because although they are annular (ring-shaped) their shape mimics that of true penannular brooches in the National Museum of Dublin. In practice it becomes difficult to distinguish brooch from pin. The reasons for the pseudo-penannular shape are unclear but they may be related to the extra strength which the decoration demanded. Among the group are some of the finest and most famous examples of Hiberno-Saxon metalwork.

The Hunterston brooch is, along with the Tara brooch, the most outstanding piece. Found in 1830 on the estate of that name in Ayrshire, it was acquired in 1891 for the national collections. As its base it has a massive, highly accomplished silver casting richly decorated with gold, silver and amber insets. All the visible silver on the front and sides has been gilded, as have the decorative panels on the back. The pin, which is free to move around the hoop, has a massive keystone-shaped head as

Bronze bell shrine of the 12th century, from Kilmichael Glassary, Argyll.

elaborately decorated as the rest of the brooch. Many of the decorative techniques, for example the animals executed in gold filigree raised on trays of sheet gold, are Anglo-Saxon although the basic shape and style of the brooch is Irish. The explanation appears to be that the brooch is the work of an Anglo-Saxon artist-craftsman employed by a native patron residing either in Ireland or western Scotland. It is possible that the motif joining the two terminals is a Christian cross and that the decorative scheme had a symbolic meaning for its owner. Certainly, it continued to be prized for several centuries following its manufacture in the 8th century AD for on the back is inscribed in Runic letters the statement 'Melbrigda owns [this] brooch'.

Brooches of this type are rare finds in Scotland but the national collections contain most of the surviving examples. None can rival the splendours of Hunterston but the fragment from Dunbeath, Caithness, comes from what must once have been a very fine brooch. Equally,

The Westness brooch, recovered from a
Viking grave on Rousay, Orkney.

the complete Westness brooch, recovered from a rich
Norse grave on the island of Rousay, Orkney, confirms
the appeal of this style of brooch for subsequent generations. Even today, the skills involved in their creation
are literally awe-inspiring.

Public utilities

The coming of the steam-powered factory, together with
the growth of the railway system, led to a massive increase
in the populations of manufacturing towns and cities
during the 19th century. This growth brought with it
horrendous overcrowding and appalling levels of disease.
In order to alleviate the worst effects of this unprece-
dented urbanization of the population, the public utilities
we now regard as indispensable, water, drainage, gas and
electricity, were developed.

The national collection relating to water and drainage is
modest, consisting of various examples of plumbing and
sanitary fittings, together with water meters and pumps
used for water supply. There are also models of such
things as water filtration equipment.

The gas collection is the largest in the field of public
utilities. The most important item is the complete gasworks which served the town of Biggar from 1839 to 1973.
This is preserved by the National Museums in association
with the Historic Building and Monuments Directorate
of the Scottish Development Department. In addition,
many items of equipment have been recovered from other
Scottish gasworks recently demolished. As with a number
of other industries, the biggest items are beyond the
resources of any museum and these, such as the continuous
vertical retort used in large works in later years, are represented by models.

The appliances used by the gas consumer are represented by collections of such things as heaters, cookers
and lights, some of which are of Scottish manufacture.

The electricity supply industry became established in
the late 19th century, and initially was solely concerned
with lighting. The Museums have early examples of Edison
and other incandescent lamps, and also the arc lamps
used for street lighting. As the supply industry developed it became increasingly important for industrial
power purposes, particularly after the electricity 'grid' was
developed in the 1930s. Unfortunately the manufacture of
electrical equipment did not flourish in Scotland to the
extent that might have been hoped for. However, there
were several important firms and they are represented in
the collection. There is an early 20th-century alternator

(alternating current generator) by the British Electric Plant Co, Alloa, and a 1920s rotary converter (alternating current to direct current) by their successors, the Harland Engineering Co. The Edinburgh firm of D Bruce Peebles is represented by a number of electric motors and generators, both full-size and model. Also in the collection are instruments and switchgear by the firm with which Lord Kelvin was associated, Kelvin & James White, of Glasgow (see **Electricity**).

Electric cookers, washing machines, refrigerators and other appliances are included in the collection and some of these are of Scottish manufacture.

Punishment
see Instruments of punishment and torture

Quaichs

Although the word 'quaich' is of Gaelic origin (from *cuach*, a cup) there is no doubt that these uniquely Scottish drinking vessels were popular in both the Lowlands and the Highlands from at least the early 17th century. They were originally shallow wooden bowls, usually with two handles or lugs. Some early examples were made out of a single piece of wood, while others were built up of sections, or

Electric lamps from the first half of the 20th century.

Stoker Lawson at work in Biggar Gasworks shortly before it was closed in 1973. *(W Lawson, Biggar)*

staves, 'feathered' together and bound with withies (twigs of willow). Alternating staves of light and dark woods, such as holly and ebony, produced a distinctive and very attractive effect. Quaichs were also made from a great variety of other materials: pewter, brass, horn and even marble, illustrated by a fine example in the Museums carved with a crowned thistle motif.

During the 17th century silver mounts were often added, and lugs engraved with initials. By the end of the century silversmiths were producing entire quaichs in silver, although they often engraved the bodies with radiating lines to imitate the earlier staves.

Quaichs were normally used for drinking and were at one time the commonest form of cup in Scotland. Their function began to change, however, and by the beginning of the 19th century they were no longer objects of daily use, having become, and remaining, popular as presentation pieces or prizes.

Renaissance jewellery
see **Medieval and Renaissance jewellery**

Reptiles: fossil

During the Permian period, about 270 million years ago (Ma), most of the small piece of the earth's crust destined to become Scotland was a hot, arid land. There were large areas of sand dunes and occasional moist places. Here and there lived various reptiles, and sometimes their footprints were preserved. The Museums have over 40 slabs of sandstone showing such fossil trackways, the majority collected by Sir William Jardine in the 1840s at Corncockle Muir, Dumfriesshire, and illustrated in his book published in 1853. Some of these animals were herbivorous dinosaurs and others were related to the ancestors of mammals.

The district around Elgin, Morayshire, has yielded later Permian footprints (from about 250 Ma) and also rare skeletal remains. Through time the bone substance itself has dissolved away, leaving only bone-shaped cavities. These have been studied by taking casts. The holes are filled with liquid rubber which, when set, is pulled out to show their original shape. Thus we can see the tusks and sturdy bones of the pig-like *Gordonia*, and the bizarre horned skull of *Elginia*. The national collections include specimens of

Wooden, staved and silver quaichs, from the late 17th to the late 19th century.

both, and the only known body skeleton of the latter.

In the late Triassic (about 220 Ma) another, more diverse reptile fauna inhabited the Elgin region, including large and small flesh- and plant-eating forms. A small lizard-like animal, *Leptopleuron*, was one of the earliest reptile discoveries in this region. Found by Patrick Duff in 1851, it became a type specimen (see **Fossils**) and is now in the National Museums together with fossils representing over half the other forms.

Later, in the Jurassic and Cretaceous periods (about 200–70 Ma) much of Scotland was inundated by shallow seas inhabited by ichthyosaurs, plesiosaurs, crocodiles and turtles. Their scattered bones occur in Skye, Eigg and near Cromarty, and many are in the collections.

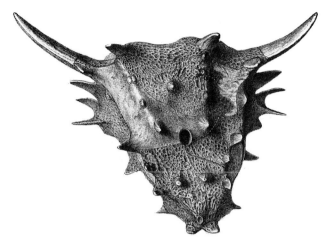

The quarry at Corncockle Muir, Dumfriesshire, showing trackways, from about 270 million years ago, winding across the rock to the right of the water. Illustrated by Jardine 1853.

Skull of *Elginia* (from about 250 million years ago) found near Elgin, Morayshire. Cast, engraved by E T Newton: 225 mm long including horn.

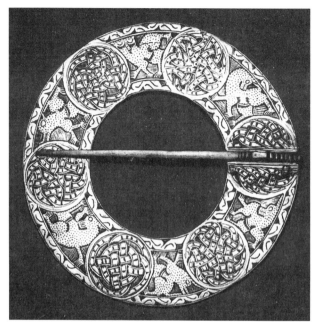

17th-century brass Highland ring brooch from Tomintoul, Banffshire.

Ring brooches

In the 13th century a new type of brooch, the ring brooch, made its appearance in Scotland and it is well represented in the collection by several hundred examples of different design and date. These brooches are normally a simple ring of bronze or silver with a free swivelling pin. The smallest and simplest may have served as buckles or for fastening undergarments. The best were meant for display and were often decorated with berries and leaves or engraved with amuletic inscriptions, often a variant in Latin of 'Jesus, King of the Jews', 'Jesus of Nazareth, King', etc. The finest example is of gold in the form of six wyverns, each gripping the one in front. Like the Bute mazer (see **Domestic silver**) it belonged to the Bannatynes of Kames in Bute and dates to about 1300.

Ring brooches have a long history in Scotland. As time went on the ring was often made broad and flat to take more decoration, like the silver-gilt brooch of about 1500 from Kindrochit Castle, Braemar, with an inscription in blundered French saying 'I am in place of a friend'. The 16th-century brooch of the MacIver-Campbells of Ballochyle has the interior filled in with a large rock crystal.

Many fine brass, or more rarely silver, ring brooches

were made in the 17th century in the Highlands for women to use in fastening their plaids. They were sometimes over 5 in (12.7 cm) in diameter with broad flat rings decorated with interlace, foliage and spotted animals. The silver ones often have inlaid niello (a black-coloured mixture of metals), and in the 18th century their manufacture was taken up by some goldsmiths working in the burghs.

Rocks

Scotland owes the great variety of its scenery to the wide range of rocks of which it is made, from the crystalline rocks of the Highlands to the soft muds and silts of the Clyde Beds and the Carse of Forth. This diversity stimulated the curiosity of scientists, and in the early 19th century Edinburgh was the centre of a key debate on the origin of rocks. The widely held view of A G Werner (1750–1817) maintained that practically all rocks, including crystalline rocks such as granite and basalt, had been deposited under water as sediments, or by precipitation from solution. Followers of James Hutton (1726–97) maintained that they were formed by heat, by the subterranean consolidation of molten matter. Hutton believed that his collection was a more effective advocate for his *Theory of the Earth* (1785) than any number of words. This collection eventually passed to Edinburgh University Museum, where it became a focus for the ill-feeling between the Huttonian and Wernerian factions. When the Wernerian Professor Robert Jameson was appointed Keeper of the Museum (1804–54) he failed to display Hutton's collection, and most if it was lost by the 1830s. Thus, although some of Hutton's collection may survive, none of it has, as yet, been traced. By 1854 the University Museum, which forms the nucleus of the present national collections, contained 40,000 rocks and minerals, many of them collected by Jameson and his followers.

The Highland and Agricultural Society was formed to promote improvement in the Highlands. It played a wider national role in urging Government to speed up the mapping of Scotland, both topographical and geological. By offering premiums, the Society ensured the early compilation of geological maps of coalfields and of counties. The geological collections formed as a necessary condition of these surveys between 1830 and 1843, included those of R J H Cunningham. He geologically mapped six mainland counties and six islands, published five papers and won four prize essay competitions, all before his untimely death at the age of 27 in 1842. Today, such collections are largely of historical interest.

There are many smaller collections of rocks, such as the economic geology specimens obtained from the Commissioners of the Great Exhibition of 1851. Another was formed by Charles Maclaren, author of *Geology of Fife and the Lothians* (1839), but better known as founder and editor of *The Scotsman*. More recently, the Museums obtained A M Cockburn's rocks which formed the basis of the first account of the geology of St Kilda (1935). These rocks were used in a major restudy of the island's geology in 1984.

For many years after 1889 part of the Museum was given over to HM Geological Survey of Scotland for a regional display of rocks, illustrating their published maps and memoirs. Most branches of petrology (the study of rocks) are represented, volcanic to deep-seated rocks, and those formed from sediments or by heat and pressure. This collection of about 7000 specimens still forms a useful reference series, and is also of historical importance. Some of the specimens have extra significance today in that they come from currently inaccessible sites, such as infilled quarries or from subsequently built-up areas.

Roman bronze tableware

The commonest forms of Roman bronze tableware are jugs, skillets and strainers, but complete decorated examples are rare in Britain. There is evidence for both religious and secular uses for the pieces: the carved scenes on Trajan's Column suggest that deep skillets were part of the regular army's kit while both jugs and skillets are common motifs on altars and officially inspired reliefs throughout the Empire. Although not all of the Scottish examples come from Roman sites, it seems most likely that they were brought in by the Roman army. Only three finds are known from north of the Antonine Wall, the frontier created on the Forth–Clyde isthmus in the middle of the 2nd century AD. Of these by far the most important is the group from Helmsdale, Sutherland, consisting of five bowls and two strainers.

The collections contain some outstanding examples of decorated pieces. Most notable among them is the enamelled skillet from West Lothian, one of the finest from anywhere in the Empire. The decorative motifs, which are executed in red, blue and green enamels, are all derived from Samian ware, a particularly fine type of Roman pottery. Enamelling is, however, a native technique and it seems likely that the small number of vessels of this type were made in Britain. Some were exported to the Continent; closely comparable pieces have been found at Maltboek in Denmark and Nehasitz in Czechoslovakia.

Bowls from the hoard found at Helmsdale, Sutherland. Only three groups of Roman material have been found north of the Roman frontier.

Two bronze wine jugs from Newstead, Roxburghshire, 1st century AD, and a rare skillet, or patera, from West Lothian, late 1st century to early 2nd century AD.

A larger and much deeper skillet is that from the native lake settlement at Dowalton Loch, Wigtownshire. Although otherwise plain it has a decorative ring-handle attached below the rim of the bowl opposite the flat handle. The movable ring is a stylized wreath ending in two monster heads and it frames a mask of Medusa. The interior has been tinned and engraved with a set of circles to aid measuring. The handle bears the stamp of the Italian bronze-founder Publius Cipius Polibius showing it to have been made in the late 1st century AD.

Jugs are the rarest of all tableware but two fine examples were found during the excavations of the Roman fort at Newstead, Roxburghshire. Both date from the late 1st century AD and were probably made in Gaul (essentially modern France). Their handles have birds' heads where they join the rim and masks where they are attached to the body, one a female head and the other the head of Bacchus.

Roman parade equipment

The classical writer Arrian describes, in his work *Tactica*, the cavalry sports, or exercises, in the Roman army. These exercises were clearly vivid spectacles, involving specially made equipment, and took the form of mock battles. The participants were 'those who have won a name for skill in horsemanship'. Some of the finest examples of this parade equipment from anywhere in the Empire were found during the excavations at the Roman fort at Newstead, Roxburghshire. Two groups, helmets and chamfrains, are represented although it is possible that some of the finer harness fittings should also be included in this category.

Arrian states that the helmets, 'unlike those made for battle, do not protect the head and cheeks alone, but conform, in every way, to the rider's face, with openings for the eyes, so contrived as to afford both safety and unimpeded vision. Fixed to the helmets are "manes", not for use, but to make a splendid show as they stream in the breeze'.

About 40 reasonably complete helmets are known and three of these, now in the National Museums, were found at Newstead. The most important is perhaps the iron face-mask and bonnet which form a virtually complete helmet. There are traces of silver-plating, which originally would have covered the whole helmet, and parts of attachments for the streamers and plumes described by Arrian. The inner surfaces show that the helmet originally had a woollen lining or padding. The second example is a brass helmet of which only the bonnet survived. It is decorated with Cupids, one of whom is driving a two-wheeled

chariot pulled by leopards. There is such a close resemblance between this helmet and one found at Nicopolis in Greece that they might both be from the same workshop. The trio of finds is completed by an exceptionally well preserved bronze face-mask.

Arrian's description of the horse fittings is less detailed but he does say that they, too, 'are well protected from the blows of opponents' javelins by chamfrains'. Although we know from other finds that some of these headpieces were made of bronze, the two leather examples from Newstead seem too elaborate for everyday use. Both were originally decorated with patterns of brass studs and it is not inconceivable that the leather was coloured by some means or other.

Roman stone sculpture

The Roman occupation of Scotland during the first centuries AD was intermittent in character and military in intent. Consequently, the surviving stone sculpture, now largely preserved in the national collections and the

Roman face-mask from Newstead, Roxburghshire, 1st century AD. One of about 40 known from the Roman Empire.

Hunterian Museum, Glasgow, wholly reflects military concerns and interests. Even the more than life-size marble head from Hawkshaw, Peeblesshire, seems best explained as part of an otherwise unknown triumphal monument erected by the Roman army in Lowland Scotland to celebrate its conquest of the area.

Many of the pieces would have incorporated inscriptions as a major element in the overall scheme. The sculpture falls into two main categories: that which is commemorative, often of a major building project, and that which is

Sculpture of Brigantia, from Birrens, Dumfriesshire, early 3rd century AD: a local goddess portrayed as the Roman Minerva.

religious. This distinction might well have been much less meaningful to the Roman soldiers than it is to us.

A good example of the links between the two categories is provided by the remarkable distance-slab found at Bridgeness, West Lothian. Similar slabs were set up along the Antonine Wall, a defensive barrier between the Clyde and the Forth begun in about 142 AD, to mark the completion of sections of the work. This particular slab, the finest of all, was found at the point where the Wall reached the Forth. The central inscription records the building of 4652 paces by the Second Legion Augusta. It is flanked by two scenes. That on the left symbolizes the Roman victories and shows a Roman cavalryman riding over four naked Britons. That on the right shows the *souvetaurilia,* a religious ceremony undertaken before important campaigns or in this case before the Wall was built. Among the onlookers is a soldier holding a flag, the earliest evidence for the use of them in Scotland.

None of the surviving religious pieces can match the ambition and size of the distance-slabs but they do compare favourably with the more usual commemorative pieces. The commonest items are altars set up to a particular god or group of gods. A good example from the fort at Birrens, Dumfriesshire, illustrates the type. Decorated with rosettes and ivy leaves, the inscription records that it was set up to Mars and the Emperor's victory by Raetian tribesman (ie from the eastern Alps) serving in the Second Cohort of Tungrians under the command of Gaius Silvius Auspex. The Roman pantheon included a large number of gods and was fully able to absorb local gods and goddesses. These were often given oriental or Roman trappings to link them to more established deities. Just such a treatment can be seen on the statue of Brigantia, also from Birrens.

Rural homes

The house and all that is associated with it is the most incisive record of life in the past. It appeals to the imagination because of the elements of contrast and continuity, and because it continues as the place of shelter, food preparation and sleep. The further back in time, the more closely was the home integrated into the fabric of farming to the point that once it was a central part of the organic cycle of animal and crop husbandry.

The national collections have a wide range of material related to rural homes. Improved farming involved a drastic rebuilding of housing, so examples of early building techniques, although well known, are rare. However, some representative samples have been collected, such as cruck (arched) frames and roof timbers, and sections of stake and rice (branch and clay) walling. Of particular importance to the home was the fireplace, as its development from a mid-floor hearth, to a gable hearth with a hanging lum, and then to a raised and ventilated hearth for coal burning, all chart vital changes in both diet and the economy. Allied to this are the means of winning fuel, peat knives, creels and barrows, and the means of cooking, from girdles, branders and pots, to bannock spades and toasters. Where possible, representative examples of all these facets have been collected. The contents of the home, such as crockery were partly dependent on available materials and local ingenuity, but were also a reflection of outside contact. The hand tools for processing wool and lint also had their place in the home (see **Man and beast**).

The collection includes recognizably 'modern' furnishing, which reflects the blending of local and more general taste. There are also bothy furnishings, such as the forms engraved with the initials of ploughmen, and their *claeser* and *mealer* kists (clothes and food chests). Besides the basic items, great importance is laid on collecting 'junk', the ephemera of everyday life that will never rate as antiques but which are vital evidence of everyday habits: the press cuttings people thought important, the pictures they cut out, even the stones they picked up in the fields because they looked 'fey' or curious. For this reason great store is laid on collecting not just individual pieces, but where possible complete rooms, from the hearth, windows and doors, to the furniture and the last oddment. This includes the evidence of pastimes and achievement: the

Carrying pails of milk with a shoulder yoke at Torphichen, West Lothian, early 20th century *(A R Jones, Edinburgh; SEA)*

fiddle, the melodeon and the Jew's harp, the plough-ing match medals, and the well-worked samplers and clootie rugs.

Working clothes are important but difficult to collect as they tend to be thrown out when their day is done. Nevertheless, the field is a wide one – from the plough-man's sark, cord breeks, nicky tams and tackety boots, to the working clothes of stalkers, keepers and shepherds, either in the estate tartans or the checks of the plaids. Persistence is steadily building this part of the collections (see **Costume**).

Rural skills and trades

The skills practised by the country population include those handed down as general knowledge, and the specialist skills which are recognized trades or occupations. Many of the general skills are inherent in farming, but others, for example the use of natural resources to make containers and ropes, and the simple but ingenious technologies to grind grain, are of more particular interest. Examples of these are represented in the national collections.

The more specialized occupations cover a wide range of activity, even within one trade such as smithing. Although there have been smiths for as long as there have been metals, smiths would not have been common before farming improvement, as metal was limited to a narrow range of items such as plough irons and the soam chain through which the large teams of draught oxen were yoked to the plough. However, with farming improvement the work of the smith increased enormously: ploughs were made to the pattern developed by James Small, horses were shod, and the ironwork vital to the new two-wheeled carts had to be provided.

It was thus natural that the smiddy was often next to the joiner's shop, where not only cart bodies and wheels were turned out, but also everything from scythe sned (handle) to simple but often elegant furniture. The range of tools associated with all these skills is very considerable, from the smith's anvils, hammers, tongs, cresses, swage blocks, callipers, etc, to the joiner's *shapes* or patterns, wheel wrighting tools, and moulding planes.

The rural building trade that developed with the virtual rebuilding of the farm steadings and housing from the 18th century onwards (see **Rural homes**) created a demand for joiners, masons, tilers, slaters and thatchers. Behind the rural building trade lay the growth of rural industries such as saw-milling, tile-making, quarrying and brick-making. All of these trades are represented by artefacts in the collections.

Muckle wheel and yarn winder in Falkland, Fife, late 19th century.
(Margaret Mercer, Ladybank; SEA)

Unique silver and silver-gilt material of native Pictish workmanship, late 8th or early 9th century, found on St Ninian's Isle, Shetland.

Some trades, such as those of the millwright and latterly the agricultural engineer, grew out of the development of particular specialities. The collection contains both evidence of these trades, for example the magnificent Breck mill from Orkney of the early 19th century, from the design of James Meikle, its inventor, and a superb range of agricultural implements.

St Ninian's Isle Treasure

The St Ninian's Isle Treasure, described as 'the most important single discovery in Scottish archaeology', consists of 28 decorated silver objects and part of the lower jawbone of a porpoise. It was found in 1958 during excavations on the site of the medieval church on St Ninian's Isle, Shetland. The treasure had been buried in a larch-wood box, seemingly below the floor of an earlier chapel. Most, if not all, of the objects are Pictish. They were buried at the end of the 8th or beginning of the 9th century, probably because of the first Norse raids and settlement.

The bulk of the treasure consists of silver bowls and brooches. Of the bowls the most elaborate is a hanging bowl, the three loops for suspension being held by the heads of animals peering over its rim. This is a well-known type of which some 150 have been found, mainly in pagan Anglo-Saxon and Viking burials. Most, however, are bronze and this is one of only three silver examples known. It was probably a century or more old when it was buried, The other seven bowls are tableware, perhaps drinking bowls. Their decoration is largely achieved through the use of punched dots, with motifs including a cross and interlaced animals as well as geometric designs.

The 12 brooches, most silver-gilt, have penannular hoops with moveable pins. Both the hoops and pins are decorated more or less elaborately in 'chip-carved' style, and have settings for coloured glass, some of which survive. Brooches of this size were probably used to fasten cloaks.

The remaining eight objects are a spoon and pronged implement, three silver-gilt cone-shaped objects with detachable perforated base plates, and a silver-gilt sword pommel and two chapes. The spoon, a unique example for this date, and pronged implement are clearly eating utensils. But there is no obvious explanation for the cone-shaped objects; they may have decorated an elaborate sword belt or shield. If this is correct they can be associated with the pommel and chapes (a fitting to strengthen the base of a scabbard). One of the chapes has inscriptions which translate as 'in the name of God the highest' and 'Resad son of Spusscio', the latter presumably referring to the owner of the sword.

It is generally assumed that the treasure belonged to a local Pictish chief and that its burial in a church does not signify that the objects were for liturgical use.

Samplers
see Embroidery

Science
see History of physical science; Modern science

Scientific instruments
see Chemical apparatus; History of physical science; Modern science

Scottish Ethnological Archive

The Scottish Ethnological Archive was begun in 1959. Started as a means of recording the changing life of Scotland's rural communities, it has developed far beyond this to include the recording of maritime, urban and industrial human activity in Scotland and of the Scots overseas. The timespan covered by the Archive has no limits, though in practice the bulk of the material dates from the late 18th century onwards.

What does the Archive collect? Photographs, slides, films, tape recordings and transcripts of information collected orally, maps, plans, drawings, etchings, prints, diaries, leaflets, posters, letters, invoices, beer mats, paper bags – anything which can help record or illustrate some sphere of human activity.

The Archive also collects newspaper cuttings and articles from periodicals which deal with any of the subjects it covers and reference is made to the objects in the collections. Notes of material held in other archives are included where possible and an effort is also made to refer to any relevant articles or books and to keep these entries up to date. For comparative purposes material from other parts of the world is also included.

Who uses the Archive? Anyone interested in family, local, social or economic history, material culture and language – from the Museums' staff preparing an exhibition or a school information pack, through those interested in a specialist topic such as thatching or forestry, to local history societies researching publications or displays

'Warning' in Gaelic, dated Dingwall 2 January 1888, against attempts by crofters to occupy the land. *(Rev Fr Charles McGregor, Banchory; SEA)*

Tommy Moffat demonstrating the old method of pulling wool at Lanark Skinnery, February 1981. *(SEA)*

RABHADH.

A CHIONN 's gun d' fhuair an Luchd-ughdarrais fios gu 'm bheil Comhchruinneachadh sluaigh, an' uine ghoirid, gu oidhirp mi-laghail a thoirt air an stoc fhuadach dheth Gabhail-fearainn Aignis, ann an Sgireachd Steornabha, agus sealbh a ghabhail air an fhearann: tha so a toirt Rabhadh gu 'm bheil cruinneachadh sluaigh air son an aobhar sin no aobhar sam bith eile dhe leithid mi-laghail agus ciontach, agus gu 'm bi na h-uile neach a ghabhas pairt ann, ged theagamh nach dean gach neach air leth foirneart, ciontach de bhi togail buaireas agus aimhreite, agus gu 'm bi iad buailteach do pheanas. Agus a thuilleadh air sin tha so a toirt Rabhadh gu 'm bheil cruinn-neachidhean de 'n ghne ud air an toirmeasg; agus ma ni sluagh an-aibreiteach mi-riaghailteac cruinneachadh, gu'n teid, a reir an "RIOT ACT," GLAODHAICH mar so a dheanamh:—"Tha ar n-ARD-BHAINTIGH-"EARNA, a' BHAN-RIGH a toirt aithne agus ordugh do 'n "t-sluagh a tha cruinn sgaoileadh gu h-ealamh, agus falbh gu "siochail a dhionnsuidh an dachaighean no chun an gnothuichean "laghail, air neo gum bi iad buailteach do na peanasan a tha air "an ainmeachadh anns an Reachd a chaidh dheanamh an "ciad bhliadhna Righ Sheorais, a chum bacadh a chuir air "iorghuillean agus cruinneachidhean aimhreiteach." "Gu'n "gleidheadh Dia a' Bhan-righ;" agus mar sgaoil cruinneachadh 'sam bith de 'n ghne ud, an taobh a stigh de dh' uair an deigh na Glaodhaich ud, bithidh gach neach a bhitheas ann ciontach de 'n chionta ud, agus buailteach do na peanasan cruaidh tha an Reachd ud ag ordachadh.

LE ORDUGH AN T-SIORRA.

TEARLACH INNES,

Inbhirfeotharan, 2mh January, 1888.   Cleireach-Siorra Siorramachd Rois.

Seal of the burgh of Crail, Fife, 16th century.

and individuals seeking to illustrate the way of life of their ancestors.

The Archive develops through fieldwork undertaken by the Museums' staff or by people working on their behalf, and to a great extent through those groups or individuals who give or lend for copying material relevant to the Archive's interests and which they wish to see preserved.

Future developments include participation in a national scheme to record life in modern Scotland, the standard-ization of subject headings to ease exchange of information with other archives and, flowing from this, the computer-ization of a section of the Archive to act as a trial run prior to computerization of all or specific types of material held.

Seals

The National Museums have nearly 200 seal matrices and a very extensive collection of electrotypes and casts of seals, including those gathered by Lt Gen Henry Hutton in the 19th century.

Seals have been in regular use in Scotland since the 12th century. In a society where most could not write they had great importance, authenticating documents as signa-tures do today. Private individuals, churches, burghs, and officers of state had matrices, normally of bronze or silver, which impressed their design in a pad of wax appended to a document. Some institutional seals were large and double sided and required the matrices to be squeezed into the wax with a screw press.

The great variety in seal design is illustrated in the collections. Kings had themselves depicted enthroned and as mounted warriors; churchmen appear in vestments; many nobles and lairds have their coats of arms. Seaports sometimes opted for ships while some churches have repre-sentations of churches. Personal seals, especially from the 16th century, were sometimes set in finger-rings, and many 18th- and 19th-century fob seals are cut in stone. Seals of all types and periods offer a fascinating insight into Scottish society and are a major artistic resource.

Semi-precious stones

Cutting and polishing can transform the most ordinary-looking rock or mineral into a sparkling, desirable stone, though semi-precious stones are of less commer-cial value and lower esteem than precious stones (see **Gems; Minerals**).

Agates occur abundantly in Scotland. They are small hard nodules of natural silica, some 2 or 3 in (5 to 8 cm)

Part of model of the engine for the *Australia* and the *Zealandia*, built by John Elder & Co, Glasgow, 1875. **Ships and marine engines**

in diameter which, when cut open and polished, commonly reveal patterns and colours of stunning beauty. Lapidaries have used these stones in jewellery, proving Scottish agates to be among the finest in the world for such purposes.

The most prolific sources of agates are the 350- to 400-million-year-old volcanic rocks in the Midland Valley of Scotland. When these rocks are decomposed by weathering the agates are released, to be found today scattered in the topsoil of farm fields, in stream beds and on beaches.

The beauty of agates led to obsessive collecting in the 19th century by, among others, Robert Miln of Woodhill, Angus, and Professor Heddle (see **Minerals**). Their collections of about 2000 agates include specimens from famous localities, such as the legendary 'Blue Hole', near Usan House, Angus, Ballindean in Perthshire, Norman's Law in Fife and Burn Anne in Ayrshire. Other additions to the national collections make it one of the finest in existence today, with almost 3000 Scottish specimens.

The origin of agate is mysterious but is being studied by scientists who are gradually revealing the complex physico-chemical series of changes that must have taken place within dense silica gels entombed in gas cavities of lavas. Agates are composed of the very fine crystalline form of silica known as chalcedony, a variety of the common mineral quartz.

The attractive, variegated red and yellow jasper from the Campsie Fells was used for the 1986 Commonwealth Games baton and in a presentation brooch to HM The Queen. A fine, cut and polished red jasper, about 16 in (40 cm) across from Craiglockhart, Edinburgh, is one of the largest semi-precious specimens in the national collections. Rhum bloodstone has been collected for centuries.

Marbles from Skye, Tiree and Iona enjoy great popularity as semi-precious stones, especially the yellow-green Iona 'stone' from which small Celtic crosses are carved. The distinctive Portsoy serpentine, utilized for innumerable *objets d'art*, and small monumental carvings, is well represented in the national collections by cut and polished slabs.

Ships and marine engines

The collection of ships and marine engines is wide ranging and includes about 200 models of merchant vessels and warships, full-size and model marine engines, engine details

The whaler *Eclipse* in the Arctic. A model of this 1867 Aberdeen-built whaler is in the collections.

The Traprain treasure: late Roman silver
and silver-gilt objects, late 4th to
early 5th century. Many pieces were
deliberately hacked up and some have
been reconstructed. **Traprain treasure**

Set of swatches of clan tartans collected
by the Highland Society of London.
Tartans

Far right example of Fair Isle knitting of
various dates. **Textiles**

Late 17th-century long guns from the
armoury of the Lairds of Grant.
Weaponry

and auxiliary machinery. Models of early ships include pre-historic Egyptian, Greek and Roman vessels, and the latest is a gas turbine-powered Royal Navy frigate of 1972.

The earliest vessel with a Scottish connection is the armed merchantman, the *Yellow Carvel*, of about 1475, sailed by the famous Largo-born Leith merchant Sir Andrew Wood. There is also a model of the warship *Great Michael* of 1511, built at Newhaven, near Edinburgh, by order of King James IV. Both models were made in the 1920s using the best information available. However, it has to be said that few details of such early vessels exist and the models are therefore somewhat conjectural.

Until the middle of the 19th century wood was the usual material for shipbuilding, although a small number of iron vessels were built earlier. One of the most important models in the collection is of a wooden shipbuilding yard, made about 1830 by a Leith shipwright.

Models of 19th-century sailing ships include one of the composite (iron frames with wood planking) clipper ship *Cutty Sark* built in 1869 at Dumbarton. The final stage of the evolution of the sailing merchant ship is well represented by very fine models of two late 19th-century Clyde-built vessels. Built of iron in 1885, the three-

masted ship *Brynhilda* came from the Linthouse yard of Alexander Stephen & Sons, while the steel four-masted barque *Glaucus* was built by Barclay Curle & Co, Glasgow, in 1889.

The early attempts to apply steam power to ship propulsion are represented by a recently made model, based on modern research, of the *Charlotte Dundas* of 1803. Designed by William Symington for use as a tug on the Forth and Clyde Canal, this had limited success, but it was an important pioneering effort.

The breakthrough in steam power came on the Clyde, and within a few decades Scotland was established as perhaps the most important shipbuilding area in the world. Her technical leadership was retained until near the end of the 19th century. Many people contributed to this but two names stand out, those of Robert Napier and John Elder.

The work of both is illustrated in the collection. An early example of an armour-clad iron warship is the *Osman Ghazi* built in 1864 by Robert Napier & Sons, Govan, for the Turkish Government. This was only five years after the first iron-clad ship, *Warrior*, now preserved at Portsmouth, and her sistership the Napier-built *Black Prince*. John Elder worked for Napier before setting up his

Model of the *Charlotte Dundas*, steamboat
built by William Symington for use on
the Forth and Clyde Canal, 1803.

own firm Randolph, Elder & Co, later John Elder & Co of Govan. In the 1850s Elder pioneered the use of the high pressure 'compound' steam engine for seagoing ships. The substantial reduction in fuel consumption, approaching 50 per cent in some cases, greatly widened the scope of the steam ship and was a major factor in the decline of the sailing ship in later years. The collection includes a model of the paddle steamer *Pacific* of 1865 and a very fine model made in the Museum Workshop of the compound engines of the SS *Zealandia* of 1875. Representing the typical steamship of the mid- to late 19th century is the very detailed large scale model of the *Nerbudda* built by William Denny and Brothers, Dumbarton, for the British India Steam Navigation Co in 1883. The model was made in the Museum Workshop from Denny drawings, and shows full details of the ship's structure, accommodation, compound engine and 'Scotch' boilers.

Evolved on the Clyde by the 1860s, as higher steam pressure came into use, the cylindrical Scotch boiler replaced the rectangular low pressure 'box' boilers previously favoured. The Museums have a full-size Scotch boiler, 14 ft (4.3 m) in diameter and 26½ ft (8 m) in length which served in the paddle steamer *Waverley* from 1947 to 1980.

At the turn of the century the steam turbine was developed for high-pressure warships, liners and cross-channel ferries. The collection includes a model of the Canadian Pacific turbine-powered liner *Empress of Scotland*, originally named *Empress of Japan* when built in 1930 by the Fairfield Shipbuilding and Engineering Co, Govan. A recent acquisition is a full-size rotor for the high-pressure turbine of the *Queen Elizabeth 2*, built by John Brown & Co, Clydebank, in 1968. This came to the Museums after the original turbine machinery was replaced by Diesel engines during the winter of 1986–7.

In addition to the seagoing ships mentioned above, the Museums have a large collection of models of Scottish and other fishing boats, lifeboats and special-purpose vessels such as dredgers. The building of dredgers was undertaken by a number of specialist firms on the Clyde who were, in their day, world leaders in the field.

Most of the models in the collection are purely exhibition models, made for display originally in the offices of the shipbuilders and the owner, or in some instances specially made for museum display. However, models are also important in ship design and a number of such models are in the collection. The most important is one made in 1826 by Robert Wilson of Dunbar, for experiments on screw propellers. It was driven by clockwork. There are also a small number of 'plating' models. These were used

Model of 'Zulu' fishing boat, as in use on the east coast of Scotland about 1930.

by shipbuilders to aid the working out of the size and shape of the hull plates.

The use of towed models to measure resistance developed in the 1880s and became standard practice. In 1882–3 William Denny & Brothers of Dumbarton became the world's first shipbuilders to construct an experiment tank for the purpose. After Denny's shipyard closed, the 100-metre-long tank was taken over by Vickers and then passed to British Shipbuilders. It finally closed in 1984 and is now preserved and maintained by the Scottish Maritime Museum. The equipment used to make the models, most of which is original, was purchased by the National Museums to secure its future, but it remains on site at Dumbarton.

Silver
see **Domestic silver; Military art; Pictish symbols; Post-Reformation church furnishings; St Ninian's Isle Treasure; Traprain Treasure; Viking silver hoards**

Snake armlets
see **Massive and snake armlets**

Snuff
see **Tobacco**

Sports and games

Not surprisingly, the sport of golf figures prominently in the Museums' collections, which have over 100 clubs of the 19th and 20th centuries. There are also outstanding game pieces, for example 11 of the Lewis chessmen and a 1691 Scottish Peers pack of cards. Other sports and games are represented sparingly, either by equipment or by trophies and medals.

In 1831 a remarkable discovery was made in Lewis of over 70 ivory chessmen, the so-called Lewis chessmen, Scandinavian work of the late 12th century. Other, later, chessmen are known as are finely-carved bone tablemen suitable for playing drafts. Chess and other board games were indulged in by the aristocracy. Cards were also a favourite diversion and a pack engraved by Walter Scott of Edinburgh in 1691 is notable for having the arms of the Scottish peers. It was not necessary, however, to have expensive boards or cards to enjoy a good game, as is shown by a stone recovered from Jedburgh Abbey with the layout for a game of merelles (not unlike noughts and crosses) scratched on it.

Other aristocratic pursuits were hawking and hunting. The former is represented in the collections by a hawking hood, used to keep the bird docile. From the 17th century shooting birds with firearms or stone bows superseded hawking in popularity.

Fifteenth-century legislation forbade the playing of golf and football so that skills in archery could be developed for use in warfare. These laws were not strictly enforced and the playing of these games flourished.

In the 18th and first half of the 19th century the golf balls in use were light and stuffed with feathers. The heads of the clubs were of hard wood and long and slender, or else iron-headed for scooping the ball out of ruts or sand. About 1850 heavier gutta-percha balls came into vogue, causing wooden clubs to be made with shorter and more rounded heads, and more resilient woods like beech and apple to be used. Gutta-percha balls were replaced at the beginning of the 20th century by balls with a rubber core.

Lewis chessmen, late 12th century, medieval tablemen, early 17th-century backgammon board and playing cards made in Edinburgh in 1691.

The 'Silver Jack', trophy of the Edinburgh Society of Bowlers, with winners' medals, 1772–84.

In many places in Scotland there was a tradition of playing football and handball, sometimes through the streets of a town, especially on Shrove Tuesday. In the collection is a ball from such games played in Jedburgh and the hand-made leather ball from the New Year's Day Ba' game of 1914 played between the 'Uppies' and 'Doonies' in Kirkwall. These ball games are still played in both towns.

Bowls was and is another favourite Scottish game, represented in the collection by the trophy of the Edinburgh Society of Bowlers of about 1771. There is evidence of curling, a version of the game played on ice, from the mid-16th century. Cannon balls were used in the game of bullets or henching, in which the balls were thrown rather than rolled as near a target as possible. Similarly quoits (metal rings) were thrown at a peg hammered into the ground.

Steam engines
see **Power for industry**

Stone axes

Ground and polished stone axes were manufactured in Britain and Ireland over a period of six millennia from

Jadeite axes, objects for display rather than tools, about 3000 BC.

around 7000 BC, remaining in use for several centuries after the introduction of metal axes. In addition to being a major tool in prehistoric woodworking (alongside stone adzes and chisels), stone axes were accorded a social and symbolic value. Individual specimens and hoards of large, unused axes may well have served as prestige goods, to be passed between individuals as valuable gifts or bridewealth; and the deliberate placing of some specimens in funerary and ceremonial monuments suggests their use as ritually significant artefacts.

Although a wide variety of rock types were utilized for axe manufacture, several preferred varieties of fine-grained or otherwise suitable stone were exploited, and the products are frequently found at considerable distances from the sources. Recent work in the Great Langdale area of the Lake District has revealed evidence for two clear strategies of rock exploitation. The first (and earliest) consisted of an *ad hoc* extraction of material, probably to meet the demands of local communities, and probably carried out as an adjunct to summer uphill pasturing. The second appears to be a much more organized, larger-scale operation designed for the export of axes; and it may be as a result of this activity that large numbers of Lake District axes found their way across the country to Yorkshire.

Axes of Great Langdale tuff have also been found in Scotland, in addition to other axes of imported material (including porcellanite from north-east Ireland and flint, probably from England). Scotland, however, possesses its own sources of good stone for axe manufacture; and one of these, at Creag na Caillich, near Killin, Perthshire, appears to have been used as a preferred source. Debris from axe manufacture can be found on the scree slope and sealed beneath peat deposits below the outcrop.

Amongst the most impressive specimens of stone axes in the collections of the National Museums are the jadeite axes. These highly polished, special-purpose items are thought to have been imported from the Continent, where several sources of the rock type are known (for example in the Italian-Swiss Alps). None of the Scottish finds comes from a datable context, but one example from Somerset was found beside a wooden trackway which dates to between 4000 and 3300 BC. Another remarkable axe, not of jadeite, is the hafted specimen found at Shulishader Point, Lewis. The haft is a perfectly preserved specimen, made of hawthorn, quince or wild apple wood, and the axe had been mounted obliquely in it to ensure maximum contact between the cutting surface and the material to be chopped.

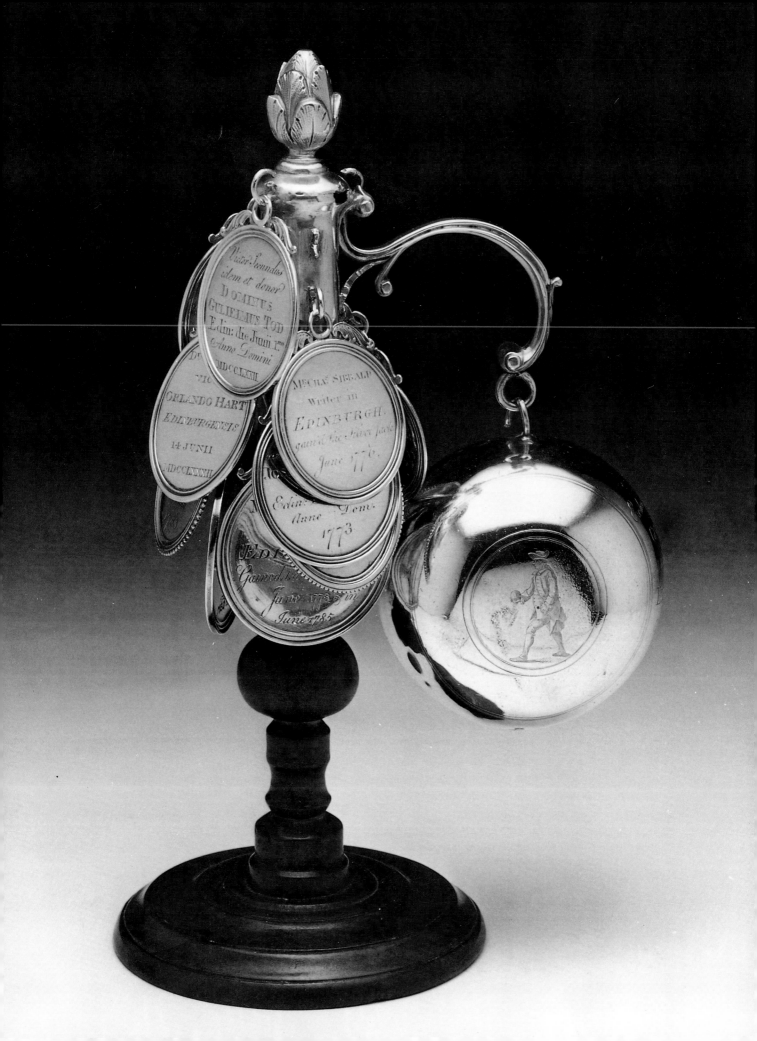

Horizontal pedestal sundial by R Melville [Glasgow], 1845. The subsidiary dials at the corners give the equivalent local time in New York, Moscow, Malabar and New Zealand.

Sundials

see also **History of physical science**

Until the mid-19th century one of the most public demonstrations of mathematical skill lay in the design and manufacture of sundials. The peculiar skill of 16th- and 17th-century Scottish stonemasons in the manufacture of multi-faceted stone dials is poorly represented in the collections of the National Museums. Quite properly most of these imposing architectural features have remained with the buildings for which they were commissioned.

There are rather more examples of the standard bronze horizontal pedestal dial. An early example made for the latitude of the Lowland belt is dated 1662 and signed 'Authore Gulielmo Havarto Mathematic'. Dating from about 1700 is a double horizontal dial by James Clerk, the engraver to the Scottish Mint. There are 18th-century horizontal dials by Joseph Williamson of Aberdeen and

George Jamieson of Hamilton, the latter advertising his work as being 'done according to astronomical rigour', and a large gnomon, the shadow-casting part of the dial, made by Robert Craig of Kilmarnock in 1744. Its surface is covered with tables of calendrical data.

From the middle decades of the 19th century the spread of the electric telegraph and the railway network emphasized the need for national time. The sundial – previously the only means by which a clock could be set – was relegated to a merely ornamental role. From this late period there is a series of horizontal dials carved from slate and calibrated to indicate noon across the globe, with subsidiary dials showing the time in places as far apart as New York and New Zealand. Their maker was Richard Melville, whose peripatetic career included a period in Glasgow.

Surveying
see **Astronomy, navigation and surveying**

Tartan

Tartan, with its myriad of colours and complexity of design, has become a symbol of nationhood, a much-prized inheritance, and a trade mark of Scotland. Its distinctive designs do not, unfortunately, have a long history. The catalogue of clan setts which are so familiar today and which define and regulate the production and wearing of tartan cloth was a creation of the 19th century. The evidence for tartan is plentiful from the 16th century as a colourful, checked cloth worn mainly in the Highlands of Scotland, but there is nothing to suggest that such a rigid system of clan tartans existed as prevails today.

Some of the oldest surviving tartans are brightly coloured and complex, indicating perhaps that in the late 17th and early 18th centuries tartan design was much in demand and the subject of much attention from weaver and wearer alike. The outfit in the National Museums of trews, jacket and plaid bought by an outsized English Jacobite in 1744 illustrates this well.

Highland dress in the mid-19th century, showing the man's belted plaid and the woman's plaid or *earasaid*.

Legal sanctions after the Jacobite Wars which culminated in the defeat of 1746 were harsh and arbitrary, especially the penalties for carrying arms and wearing Highland dress; the Disarming Act of 1746 identified tartan as the uniform of Jacobitism and symbol of treachery. Although this measure remained in force until 1782, tartan survived among families who had avoided involvement in the Jacobite cause and more especially as the dress of Highland units in the British Army (see **Military uniform**). Fear and distrust of the Highlands turned rapidly in the 1760s to fascination and enthusiasm. This ensured that the Highlander, a focus of interest of European Romanticism, was transformed from brigand and traitor into the heroic manifestation of primitive virtues.

Tartan as the design and inspiration of the kilt was revived in the 19th century as the epitome of the dress of the Highlanders and came to be adopted as the national dress of all Scots, whether Lowland or Highland.

The collection of samples of tartan begun by the Highland Society of London in 1816 established the convention that the clan tartan was that endorsed or ordained by the chief of a name. The process of collection and research carried out by the Highland Society in the 19th and 20th centuries established an archive of over 600 tartan samples which are now in the care of the National Museums.

Apart from colour and design, the essence of tartan is display. George IV's visit to Scotland in 1822 created a vogue for tartan by its pageantry. One or two costumes from this pageantry are in the National Museums' collections and demonstrate the evolution of tartan from functional dress to costume of a theatrical style.

The collections include the evidence in the form of several thousand letters and swatches of the tartan-weaving firm of William Wilson and Sons of Bannockburn near Stirling. In business as early as 1724, their records survive from 1765 and show that from then until the mid-19th century they monopolized the supply of tartan cloth to the army and fed the increasing demand of an eager public for tartan. Wilsons of Bannockburn not only manufactured tartan, they also arranged setts, colours and shades of colour according to taste and demand rather than any codes.

The enthusiasm for tartan in the 1820s inspired books in the 1830s and 1840s whose researches attempted to explain and delimit the history of tartan in terms of an exclusively Highland antiquity. Homely and exotic fabrics were made in tartan both in Scotland and abroad, and the collections of the National Museums, in the form of crinolines and flowing ballgowns, full evening dress and costume, and fashion plates themselves, illustrate the great success achieved by tartan.

Textile, paper and printing industries
see also Textiles

There is a tendency to think of Scottish industry in terms of coal, steel and shipbuilding. Yet even during the 19th century when these industries were at their peak, they did not represent anything approaching the whole of Scottish industry.

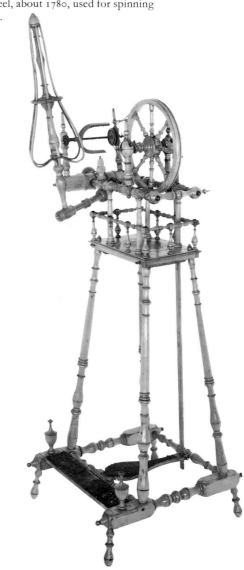

Boudoir or drawing room spinning wheel, about 1780, used for spinning flax.

The textile industry in particular was a very large employer in almost every part of the country, and even today, despite reductions in size, it is still a much larger and more important industry than is generally realized. Wool, cotton, flax, jute and silk were all processed in Scotland and the national collections include equipment used for each of them.

A large collection of spinning wheels and a number of hand looms represent the earlier unmechanized industry, which flourished until the early 19th century. A particularly important specimen is a very fine early 19th-century hand loom used for silk weaving in Lanarkshire. From the post-Industrial Revolution industry there are machines by a number of the leading Scottish makers, including 20th-century jute-spinning machinery by J F Low of Monifieth, and power looms for cotton and linen by the Anderston Foundry Co, Glasgow and the Dunfermline Foundry Co. After weaving, cloth was further processed to clean and finish it to meet the customers' needs. The collection includes an early 19th-century 'beetling engine' used on some types of linen and a 'milling machine' for washing and shrinking woollen cloth.

Cotton fabric was often printed with decorative patterns. Printing was originally carried out with hand printing blocks, one for each colour, before the development of machine printing. The collection includes examples of both hand blocks and the printing rollers used in the machines.

As with the textile industry, paper-making was originally a craft industry which was later mechanized. Moulds and other equipment used for hand-made paper are represented in the collections. When the industry became mechanized the scale of the equipment changed dramatically. Although there are a few full-size machine components, it is the models that make up the most important part of the collection. Among these is a large 19th-century model of a complete paper-making machine, built for the Industrial Museum of Scotland (see *page 9*) by Bertrams of Edinburgh.

Printing was a major Edinburgh industry which led to the formation of a number of important printing machinery manufacturers. Notable among these Edinburgh firms were D & J Greig, Miller & Richard, Thomas Long, and the Leith Walk Foundry, all of which are represented in the collection. Major items are a 'Columbian' hand press by Greig, supplied originally to the Industrial Museum of Scotland for label printing, and the rotary printing press shown by Thomas Nelson at the Great Exhibition in London in 1851.

Textiles
see also **Costume; Tartan; Textile, paper and printing industries**

The textile collections represent a wide range of techniques and materials, with examples for both domestic furnishings and for clothing.

The woven textiles cover a great variety of materials. The collection's earliest examples are fragments from archaeological excavations, which help to build up a picture of the range of fabrics available in the past. More recent material includes early 20th-century sample books from Border mills. Other interesting pieces are samples of tweed from St Kilda and a length of Harris tweed woven by Miss Marion Campbell in 1988, as well as blankets and coverlets from various parts of Scotland.

Printed textiles include the important Levenfield print books of the late 18th century showing the range and quality of printed cottons and linens produced at that time. A huge collection of samples from the Turkey Red printed

Turkey Red print for use on a sari border or a shawl, about 1860. Probably from Archibald Orr Ewing's factory, Vale of Leven, Dunbartonshire.

White linen wall hanging embroidered in silks and wools with a crown and a cipher, 'IRCR, 1719', for the marriage of James Stuart and Clementina Sobieska.

The Petrie family of Lerwick, Shetland dressing shawls, early 20th century.

cotton industry in the Vale of Leven show the trade goods which were exported in the 19th century.

Another very important industry in Scotland was that of linen. The collection includes homespun and woven examples and a series of white damask table napkins, woven with the names of owners and with dates ranging from 1700 to 1775. These seem to be a uniquely Scottish trend, although many of the designs are copied from Dutch and Flemish sources.

Fair Isle, Shetland and Sanquhar knitting and fisherman knits are also to be found in the collection, some of them acquired as early as the mid-19th century. By way of comparison there are examples from the Faroes and the Balkans. Machine knitwear from various well-known companies was collected in the 1970s and it is hoped that this aspect can be extended.

The French and English silk looms supplied many Scots people with the fabric for their grand *toilettes*; there is a good range of silks in the collection. Hand-made lace from New Pitsligo is represented, and machine laces from Darvel, Ayrshire. Lace can also be seen on many of the dresses in the collection.

Tapestries and modern hangings include a representative selection from the Edinburgh Tapestry Company. There are also several tapestries from an earlier European tradition, including one of the Decius Mus series designed by Rubens and woven in Flanders in the early 17th century.

Surprises sometimes occur, as when the only documented products of the Edinburgh shawl industry came to light. Happily these were acquired for the collection and fill in yet another piece of the jigsaw that is the textile heritage of Scotland.

Tobacco

The tobacco habit was probably imported into Scotland from England early in the 17th century. The first reference to the 'weed' in Scotland is in 1606 and the earliest references to clay tobacco pipes date to around the same time. Smoking became an integral part of the social scene, and pipes, which seem originally to have been imported from Holland, were being made by an increasingly large number of manufacturers in Edinburgh, Glasgow and elsewhere.

The large collection of Scottish-made pipes in the National Museums demonstrates that there was a progressive change of shape and size of the bowls,

starting with small, sloping bowls in the early 1600s, and moving eventually to larger upright types by the late 19th century. In the 18th century there was a decline in smoking, and consequently in pipe production. Both revived again in the 19th century.

The decline in smoking was possibly caused by the huge increase in snuff-taking. The philosopher Dugald Stewart claimed that snuff had civilized the Scottish race! Snuff-taking certainly produced a wide range of associated paraphernalia: mills (for grinding), mulls, boxes, brushes, horns and spoons, all of which are well represented in the collection.

One of the earliest designs of a snuff container, or mull, was the lidded vase or baluster form. These elegant mulls are found in various materials such as silver, horn, ivory and ebony. The most distinctive combine contrasting materials in alternating staves and are similar in construction to some quaichs (see **Quaichs**). Curly sheep or cow horns were also commonly used to make mulls. Complete cow horns, usually mounted and decorated with

Horn snuff mull of the Incorporation of Taylors of the Canongate: the silver mounts were added by successive deacons and treasurers between 1769 and 1802.

Wooden snuff box with pen and ink
illustration from Burns' 'Tam O'Shanter',
by Sliman of Catrine, Ayrshire, early 19th
century.

and diversified into the production of all sorts of wooden souvenirs, which attracted the generic term 'Mauchline ware', although it was also made elsewhere. These trinkets ranged from tartan book covers to napkin rings decorated with transfer-printed topographical scenes.

Trade tokens
see also **Banknotes; Coins**

In the second half of the 18th century the progress of the Industrial Revolution and the developing British economy produced an increased demand for low value coinage, with which to pay the workforce and buy goods. Unfortunately, the government failed to issue an adequate amount of small change, causing serious hardship to a large number of the working population. One remedy for this was for traders and companies to issue their own token coinage. These tokens circulated locally and could be used to buy goods or could be redeemed by their issuers for regal coinage.

silver, would be used for the large communal mulls which circulated at the dinner table.

These large mulls often belonged to corporate bodies such as the Trades Incorporations, and the Museums have a fine example which belonged to the Incorporation of Taylors of the Canongate, decorated with silver bands added by successive Deacons and Treasurers of the craft.

Perhaps the most interesting Scottish snuff containers are the wooden boxes developed in the late 18th century. These were made mainly of plane tree or elm, although other woods were also used. The prerequisite for a good snuff box is a tight lid to keep the snuff dry, therefore the wooden boxes needed a well-made close-fitting hinge. The credit for the invention of the mechanization of cutting these integral hinges goes to a bedridden clock-maker in Alyth, James Sandy. His work was developed by Charles Stiven of Laurencekirk who began cheap, commercial production. Others soon followed and box-making became a prosperous industry in Kincardineshire and especially in Ayrshire.

One of the most famous manufacturers was the firm of W & A Smith of Mauchline. They produced, as did many others, a wide range of decorative finishes on their boxes. Some of the most attractive have pen-and-ink coats of arms, sporting scenes or episodes from popular literature, such as the lively depiction of Cutty Sark's dance from Tam o' Shanter on a box in the Museums' collection. Smith's became the largest manufacturer and developed a mechanical process for transferring designs from the original on to the boxes. They outlasted the mania for snuff

Copper and lead tradesmen's tokens *right*
and countermarked silver dollars *left*,
late 18th and early 19th centuries.

The 'ordinary' bicycle or 'penny farthing', of the 1890s, and a Strida bicycle of 1988.

It has been estimated that between 1787 and 1817 over 10,000 different types of token were produced. They were issued mainly in farthing or halfpenny denominations, although some pennies were also produced. They varied in quality from very crude lead disks stamped only with the issuer's initials, such as one marked 'WF' from Leith, to masterpieces of the die-sinkers art, with vivid depictions of industrial or commercial scenes. The copper halfpenny showing the Dundee Glassworks and one issued by Campbell's snuff shop in Edinburgh are fine examples. All of these are in the National Museums, which have a comprehensive collection of tokens. Such was the contemporary fascination with tokens that they immediately became collector's items and in fact some were issued solely for this reason.

The shortage of official small change was eased in 1799 when Boulton and Watt produced their 'Cartwheel' issue of copper coins. Production of tokens tailed off at this time, although it revived again in the first quarter of the 19th century until they were finally declared illegal in 1817. Thereafter traders continued to issue tokens only for advertising and not as an alternative currency.

Another way round the scarcity of coinage was the issue of countermarked silver dollars. During the continental wars of the early 19th century large quantities of Spanish and French silver coins were captured. These were reissued in Scotland after they had been marked with the name of the issuer and their value, normally 4s 9d (23p) or 5s (25p). The Museums have a good collection of these, circulated by such companies as the New Lanark cotton works, the Deanston Cotton Mill and the Thistle Bank in Glasgow.

Trades
see **Rural skills and trades**

Transport

Transport is a popular subject and many organizations have been actively collecting in the field. The National Museums saw no need to compete, but devoted the available resources to equally important but less immediately popular areas. Nevertheless, good collections have gradually been built up. The bulk of the material has a Scottish provenance although manufactured elsewhere, but there are a number of very important Scottish-built items.

The oldest surviving Scottish-built railway locomotive, built by Hawthorn of Leith in 1861, is in the collection.

It spent all its working life shunting at collieries in Lancashire. The Museums also have one of the last steam shunting locomotives to be built: it was made in 1953 by Andrew Barclay, Sons & Co, Kilmarnock, for the National Coal Board. The most important of the model locomotives is *Abbotsford*, one of a class of 4-4-0 express locomotives introduced in 1876 by the North British Railway. Built in the railway's own works at Cowlairs, to the design of Dugald Drummond, these machines influenced British locomotive practice for 50 years. As none survive, the model and the drawings from which it was built in the Museum Workshop are particularly important.

As with a number of other 20th-century industries, motor vehicle manufacture always seemed rather precarious in Scotland. The most successful firm was Albion Motors of Glasgow, who at an early stage moved entirely into commercial vehicles. There is a very good example of a private car produced by the firm in 1900.

The aircraft and airship collection is based at the Museum of Flight, East Fortune. The airship era began with the hot air balloons, few of which have survived. However, the Museum has material connected with hydrogen-filled airships. There are models of First World War non-rigids, for example the Coastal, Coastal Star and North Sea Class. Of particular note are items from the rigid R34 which flew in 1919 from East Fortune airfield to Mineola, New York, and back. This was built by Beardmores.

The aircraft collection begins with the hang glider, Percy Pilcher's *Hawk*, from the late 19th century. There are several engines of about 1910, including the Wright B, the 35 hp Green and the Arrol-Johnston engine made in Paisley in 1911 and used by Graham Donald in a Bleriot aircraft.

The aircraft industry in Scotland has remained small with most of the early examples being built in garages. In the 1930s Weir of Cathcart built autogiros and experimented with helicopters. Their W2 autogiro is in the collection. Scottish Aviation, based at Prestwick, is represented by a Twin Pioneer built in 1959 and the Bulldog, built in 1969.

Traprain Treasure

The Traprain Treasure, which consists of Roman silver plate, was found in 1919 during excavations of a major native settlement on Traprain Law, East Lothian. It weighs over 54 lb (24 kg) and includes pieces from more than 150 different objects. The treasure was packed tightly

together in a pit and, to judge from the four silver coins, it was buried around AD 410–425. Very few objects were whole; most had been cut into pieces and flattened, and some objects are represented only by fragments.

Although we do not know where any of the objects was made, silver of this quality was produced at a number of workshops in both the western and eastern Empire – in Rome, Trier, Constantinople and Antioch, for instance. While the items may have come from southern Britain as payment for mercenaries defending the frontier, it is equally possible that they represent loot acquired by British raiders on the Continent.

There are four main groups of objects. By far the largest is table silver, which includes wine jugs and goblets, bowls, dishes and spoons. Some of the bowls and dishes are plain but others are decorated and enhanced with gilding and niello (a black metal compound) inlay. The motifs show scenes of gods, goddesses and heroes such as Venus, Pan and Hercules, and of animals as well as various foliage and geometric patterns. The range of styles indicates that the pieces are the products of several workshops.

The second largest group comprises objects with Christian iconography, presumably part of the church plate of an early Christian community. The group includes flasks, strainers and spoons, the latter perhaps as likely to belong to a Christian household as a church. Among this group is an outstanding silver-gilt flask decorated with four biblical scenes, Adam and Eve, the Adoration by the Three Wise Men, and Moses Striking the Rock; the fourth scene has long been considered to be the Betrayal of Christ by Judas but it has recently been suggested that it is another episode from the life of Moses, the miracle of the quails in the desert.

The other two groups are both small. The items from a lady's toilet set include parts of two mirrors and silver jars for ointments. Finally, there are parts of an officer's military uniform, strap fittings and buckles reflecting Germanic taste. The officer in question may have come from, or been stationed in, eastern Europe since two of the objects are of types found only in present-day Hungary.

Tweed
see **Textiles**

Viking goldwork

Neck-rings, arm-rings and finger-rings of gold and silver form one of the most important elements in Viking jewellery. In Scotland and elsewhere silver rings also acted as a convenient method of storing and transporting bullion, and many were cut up as required for trading purposes. Gold rings no doubt provided a similar means of storing bullion, but there is less evidence from Scotland of Viking gold jewellery being used for commercial transactions. The only example of Viking goldwork which has been deliberately cut up is part of an arm-ring that was found with three incomplete gold ingots and six complete gold finger-rings in the Hebrides during the last century. This remarkable hoard which could reflect the work of either a goldsmith or a merchant is in the national collections. It would seem that goldwork, which was undoubtedly scarce, was treasured for more than just its trading value.

The most recent piece of Viking goldwork to join the collection is the gold arm-ring from the Sound of Jura. This pleasing piece of 10th-century jewellery is formed from two twisted gold rods which merge with a flat band of gold decorated with stamped ornament. The only other example of a complete gold arm-ring from Scotland is that from the Island of Oxna, Shetland, which is also in the national collections. What makes the discovery of the Jura Sound arm-ring even more remarkable, and fortuitous, is the fact that it was found on the sea-bed by skin-divers. Precisely how it came to be lost at sea must remain a matter for speculation.

Many Viking-period gold finger-rings also make use of the decorative effects of twisted or plaited gold wire. There are a number of these in the national collections, but amongst the most striking are the finger-rings from the Hebrides already mentioned and another plain gold

Viking gold armlet, 10th century, found by skindivers in the Sound of Jura.

ring from Fladda Chuinn also in the Hebrides. From the Northern Isles have come a set of four gold rings from Stenness, in Orkney, and a single gold ring from Whalsay, Shetland. Two of the Stenness rings are made from plaited and twisted wire as is the Whalsay example. The other two gold rings from Stenness are relatively plain, being made from a single tapered band of gold.

Viking ships

Vikings are and were identified as much by their ships as by their behaviour, but tangible remains of their ships are extremely rare. Constructed mainly from wood, they require exceptional circumstances of preservation to survive. The national collection has, however, a range of remarkable and evocative survivals from the age of the Viking ship.

From midden deposits surrounding mid-9th-century Viking houses at Jarlshof, on the southern tip of Shetland, come simple drawings of ships scratched on laminates of sandstone by the Vikings themselves. Some show the classic Viking long-ship with high prow and stern, oarsmen and steering oar, mast and rigging. Others provide details of such terrifying Viking ship imagery as the dragon's head ship-prow.

Exceptional evidence of Viking seamanship and skill in boatbuilding has also been found in the Western Isles. Two wooden stem-posts for a clinker-built boat were found in a bog on the island of Eigg in the 19th century. One is finished and the other has been roughed out ready

Depiction of a Viking trading vessel, 9th–11th century, from Jarlshof, Shetland, a major Viking site.

for final working. The posts have been buried in order to help condition the wood. Their method of manufacture with a V-shaped cross-section and stepped edges, to which the strakes (which make up the sides of the boat) would have been attached with clinker nails, is classically Scandinavian. The Eigg stem-posts compare very closely with those from the wreck of a lightly built cargo-vessel, of about 44 ft (13.5 m) in length, found at Skuldelev, Denmark.

For many years the remains of smaller Viking boats (approximately 16 ft (5 m) in length) of the 'færing' type have been recovered in crude detail from boat burials. Some of the most important Viking grave goods in the national collections, such as those from Oronsay and Kiloran Bay, Colonsay, come from boat burials. In recent years improvements in excavation techniques have permitted work on burials to reveal the ghostly impression of such boats in the ground. The National Museums have taken the opportunity of one such excavation at Westness, Rousay, Orkney, to make an exact replica of the ghost vessel used to bury a 9th-century Viking man complete with his weapons and tools.

Viking silver hoards
see also **Viking goldwork**

About 30 Viking silver hoards, mostly mixtures of objects and coins in varying proportions, have been found in Scotland. Some are now lost and known only through contemporary records of their discovery. Of the survivors the vast majority are in the national collections.

Most have been found in north and west Scotland which was the heartland of Norse settlement. Even though the overall number of hoards is small, especially in comparison with Ireland where five times as many are recorded, some are substantial finds. In particular, the Skaill hoard with well over 100 objects and a bullion weight in excess of 17 lb (8 kg) bears comparison with the biggest hoards from anywhere in the Viking world.

Although a few hoards deposited in the 9th century contain Norse objects, the other items in them suggest that they should not be viewed as Viking hoards. Most of the true Viking hoards were buried in the period between the middle of the 10th and the first half of the 11th century. Their occurrence suggests that wealth from trade was at this time concentrated in the Norse areas, even if those regions did not enjoy the rich commercial relations with England and the Continent available to the Irish settlers. Nevertheless, items such as the Arabic coins from as far afield as Baghdad, which are found in the hoards, indicate the extensive Viking trading networks to which Scottish settlements had access at this period.

Many of the objects in the hoards have been cut up into pieces and are represented only by fragments. This indicates that their primary value was as silver bullion. However, in the larger hoards, and especially that from Skaill, Orkney, complete objects such as brooches, arm-rings and neck-rings do occur. Indeed, the large 'thistle brooches' in the Skaill hoard, which all appear to be the work of a single craftsman, are outstanding examples of Viking art.

One particular type of object, the plain arm-ring or 'ring money', well illustrates the problems of determining whether an item had value in its own right or merely as bullion. The arm-ring is the commonest type in the Scottish hoards and there has long been a suggestion that it represents a form of currency in an otherwise essentially coinless society. The evidence from weight and size is not, however, conclusive and they may just be relatively simple arm-rings.

Watercolours
see **Military art**

Weaponry

The National Museums have over 1000 weapons used by the Scots from medieval times, in addition to regulation issues by the armed forces (see **Military weapons**). The collections owe much to the scholarship and generous 1940 bequest of Charles Whitelaw, and to the gift of the collection of N C R Colville. In 1977 the important private armoury of the Lairds of Grant (Earls of Seafield) was acquired. It contains half (13) of the surviving 17th-century Scottish long guns. There is practically no surviving medieval armour though the collections contain some 17th-century pieces.

In the Middle Ages the sword was the pre-eminent weapon. From the late 15th century to the early 17th century some swords were so large that they could only be used with two hands. The sword blades were imported from Germany but the hilts were normally made by Scottish armourers. In the Highlands swords were made with drooping guards and decorative rings at the ends in the form of quatrefoils. These are the claymores (from the Gaelic for great sword) so feared by generations of Lowlanders and Englishmen alike.

Before the 16th century swords may have been owned by few apart from the nobles and lairds. They had simple cross-guards giving little protection to the hand and wrist, but in the 16th century Scottish armourers started making basket hilts which enclosed the hand. These were fitted with broad blades for slicing and cutting. By the 17th century they were being made in large quantities in the Lowland towns. The best were produced in Glasgow and Stirling in the 18th century. The bars and panels forming the hilts were decoratively shaped and pierced, and the very best were inlaid with gold, silver or brass wire. Some of the armourers, for example John Allan of Stirling and his sons John and Walter, and the Simpsons of Glasgow, stamped their hilts with their initials.

Highland targes are circular, made of wood covered with leather, and about 20 in (51 cm) in diameter. They were held by straps over the lower left arm. Targes have a long ancestry, being little different from the shields used by the Vikings, but in the 17th century the Highlanders lovingly ornamented them with brass or silver nails and bosses, and tooled the leather with leafy scrolls, interlace and little spotted animals.

The dirk, also favoured by Highlanders, is a dagger with a long pointed blade, sharp on one side only, and a small, normally wooden, grip. They had many uses, domestic as well as warlike. The Museums also have examples of 19th-century dirks set with silver mounts and jewels, and smaller, similarly ornamented knives called skean-dhu (from the Gaelic for black knife). These were purely for decoration.

More refined than dirks were the dudgeon daggers made in Edinburgh in the early 17th century. They have slender pointed blades, gilded and engraved with decoration including inscriptions, for example, 'MY HOPE AND TRIEST IS IN YE LORD'. Their hilts are of polished wood. They were essentially for wear by the upper classes with civilian clothing.

From the late 16th century gun-makers in towns such as Edinburgh and Dundee were manufacturing pistols. These were finely crafted prestige objects, typically made entirely of metal, either brass or iron. In the early years of the industry brazil wood or fruit wood was also used. The triggers lack any guard and there is a long hook on one side of the stock so that they can be hung on a belt, normally in pairs. Stocks, barrels and locks are richly decorated with engraving and inlaid wire and plaques.

Many gunsmiths have been identified since they put their initials or name on their work. The collection has outstanding brass pistols and a brass long gun by

James Low of Dundee, from the early 17th century. By the late 17th century gunsmiths are found working in many small towns. Gunsmiths in Doune, Perthshire a particularly important centre, included four generations of the Caddell family, all called Thomas, John and Alexander Campbell, and John Murdoch.

Long guns were also made by Scottish gunsmiths from the 16th century, and in the 18th and 19th centuries many fine sporting guns were produced. The glory of the National Museums' collections is a group of distinctively Scottish 17th-century sporting guns. Most, including a group which belonged to the Lairds of Grant, have fluted, paddle-shaped butts. They were worked upon by the Grants' clan armourer, William Smith of Duthil, Inverness-shire.

In the late 17th and early 18th century craftsmen working in the north-east and Highlands made powderhorns out of cows' horns. These were flattened and decorated all over, sometimes with designs similar to those on the targes.

The Scots also manufactured artillery. It was James III who first started casting pieces of artillery in Edinburgh in the 1470s, and in the 16th century there was a gun foundry in Edinburgh Castle. Guns were either cast in bronze or made up of hoops and bands of wrought iron. They were heavy and difficult to manoeuvre but in the middle of the 17th century James Wemyss, relying on experience gained in the Swedish army, developed so-called leather cannon – guns with a light metal core tightly bound with cord and leather. They were used with the Scottish armies in 1650 and 1651. In the late 18th and early 19th century the famous Carron Ironworks near Falkirk produced carronades of various sizes, guns favoured by the British navy and also by Wellington in his land campaigns in Spain.

Weights and measures

Lord Swinton's *Proposal for Uniformity of Weights and Measures in Scotland* of 1779 opens: 'The advantages of uniformity in weights and measures are so great, and so general, that it has been an object of the legislature in every commercial kingdom.' Definitions of weight, length and volume were enshrined in statute from the reign of David I (1124–53). The basic units were first defined as the penny weighing 32 grains of good round wheat, the inch

Pair of brass pistols made by James Low of Dundee, 1611, from the collection of Louis XIII of France.

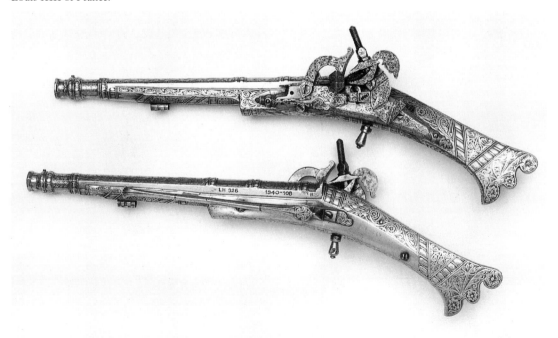

the length of three barleycorns without the tails and the gallon to be made up of four pounds of sea-water, four of standing water and four of pure river water.

Subsequent legislation attempted more precise definitions and also reflected custom and practice. Under the revised legislation of 1616 the primary standards were themselves dispersed. The stone of 16 pounds troy was held by Lanark, the Scots or Stirling pint by Stirling, the firlot dry capacity measures by Linlithgow and the ell linear measure by Edinburgh. This situation tended to encourage local variations in measurement.

Under the 1707 Act of Union English weights and measures were to be introduced. The collection includes Queen Anne liquid and dry measures and weights, supplied as secondary standards to the Burgh of Linlithgow The measures were approved at Stirling, the weights at Lanark. At first the legislation was largely ignored, and Scots measures continued to be used, with English measures gaining only a tenuous foothold. Lord Swinton's concern with the variety of commercial standards used throughout Scotland in the late 18th century was not reflected in further legislative action for over 50 years.

The collection contains examples of local Imperial standards supplied to Scottish burghs in and after 1824. A number of these are of special interest because they were used in the early 1830s for comparison with existing Scottish standards before they were legally abolished in 1836. In spite of the formal introduction of Imperial measures across the United Kingdom and the British Empire after 1824, the earlier standards of measurement continued for some time. There is an example of a wooden Scots forpit, the fourth part of a peck, verified in 1861, despite the fact that this capacity measure ceased to have legal standing in 1707.

Wildlife
see **Natural History Collections**

Woodwork
see **Carved and painted woodwork of the 16th and 17th centuries**

Zoology
see **Natural History Collections**

Scottish weights and measures dating from 1707–1861.

BOOK LIST

This list includes books that may be helpful to readers wishing to find out more about topics covered in this volume, and publications that provide information specifically on the National Museums' Scottish collections. Most are either in print or should be available in public libraries.

Books are grouped under category headings and are listed in alphabetical order by author. Those with asterisks are published by or in association with the National Museums of Scotland. Enquiries about these titles can be made to the Museums' Publications Officer.

Historical and cultural background

Barrow, G W S. *The Kingdom of the Scots*, London, 1973.

Bell, A S (ed). *The Scottish Antiquarian Tradition: Essays to Mark the Bicentenary of the Society of Antiquaries of Scotland and its Museum, 1780–1980*, Edinburgh, 1981.

Breeze, D J (ed.) *Studies in Scottish Antiquity Presented to Stewart Cruden*, Edinburgh, 1984.

Bryden, M. *Corn Rigs and Barley Rigs*, Spotlight Pack, Edinburgh, 1986.

Calder, J (ed). *The Enterprising Scot*, Edinburgh, 1986.

Calder, J. *The Story of the Scottish Soldier 1600–1914: Bonny Fighters*, Edinburgh, 1987.

Cheape, H and I F Grant. *Periods of Highland History*, London, 1987.

Cowan, E J (ed). *The People's Past*, Edinburgh, 1980.

Daiches, D (ed). *A Companion to Scottish Culture*, London, 1981.

Dickinson, W C. *Scotland from Earliest Times to 1603*, Edinburgh, 1961.

Fenton, A. *Scottish Country Life*, Edinburgh, 1976.

Fenton, A. *The Shape of the Past: Essays in Scottish Ethnology*, vols 1 & 2, Edinburgh, 1985.

Fenton, A. *Country Life in Scotland. Our Rural Past*, Edinburgh, 1987.

Fenton, A, D Kidd, E Langler and C Hendry. *The Scottish Ethnological Archive*, Edinburgh, 1988.

Ferguson, W. *Scotland 1689 to the Present*, Edinburgh, 1968.

Hazell, K. *Not Just Haggis*, Spotlight Pack, Edinburgh, 1986.

Kay, B. *Odyssey, Voices from Scotland's Recent Past*, Edinburgh, 1980.

Kay, B. *Odyssey, Voices from Scotland's Recent Past: the Second Collection*, Edinburgh, 1982.

Lenman, B. *An Economic History of Modern Scotland*, London, 1977.

Mackie, J D. *A History of Scotland*, 2nd edition, Harmondsworth, 1969.

Menzies, G (ed). *Who Are the Scots?* London, 1971.

Mitchell, A. *The Past and the Present*, Edinburgh, 1880.

Mitchison, R. *A History of Scotland*, London, 1970.

O'Connor, A and D V Clarke. *From the Stone Age to the Forty-Five: Studies Presented to R B K Stevenson*, Edinburgh, 1983.

Smout, T C. *A History of the Scottish People 1560–1830*, London, 1969.

Smout, T C. *A Century of the Scottish People 1830–1950*, London, 1986.

Stevenson, D and W B Stevenson. *Scottish Texts and Calendars. An Analytical Guide to Serial Publications*, Edinburgh, 1987.

Symm, J. *Scottish Farming Past and Present*, Edinburgh, 1988.

Thomson, D S (ed). *A Companion to Gaelic Scotland*, Oxford, 1983.

Wood, S. *The Scottish Soldier*, Manchester, 1987.

Review of Scottish Culture, I (1984), II (1986), III (1987) and IV (1988).

In addition, the *Proceedings of the Society of Antiquaries of Scotland* (1857–present) are an invaluable source of information on Scottish material culture.

Archaeology

Breeze, D J, D V Clarke and G Mackay. *The Romans in Scotland*, Edinburgh, 1980.

Childe, V G. *Scotland Before the Scots*, London, 1946.

Clarke, D V, T Cowie and A Foxon. *Symbols of Power at the Time of Stonehenge*, Edinburgh, 1985.

Close-Brookes, J. *St Ninian's Isle Treasure*, Edinburgh, 1981.

Close-Brookes, J and R B K Stevenson. *Dark Age Sculpture*, Edinburgh, 1982.

Cowie, T. *Magic Metal. Early Metalworkers in the North-East*, Aberdeen, 1988.

Henderson, Isabel. *The Picts*, London, 1967.

Piggot, S (ed). *The Prehistoric Peoples of Scotland*, London, 1962.

Piggott, S. and K Henderson. *Scotland Before History*, London, 1958.

Ralston, I and J Inglis. *The Picts in the North East and Their Background*, Aberdeen, 1988.

Ritchie, A. *Scotland BC*, Edinburgh, 1987.

Ritchie, A and G Ritchie. *Scotland: Archaeology and Early History*, London, 1981.

Robertson, A. *The Antonine Wall*, Glasgow, 1972.

Arts and material culture

Apted, M R. *Painted Ceilings of Scotland*, Edinburgh, 1966.

Burnett, C J and H Bennett. *The Green Mantle*, Edinburgh, 1987.

Calder, J. *If It Wasnae for The Weaver*, Spotlight Pack, Edinburgh, 1986.

Caldwell, D H. *The Scottish Armoury*, Edinburgh, 1978.

Caldwell, D H. *Scottish Weapons and Fortifications*, Edinburgh, 1981.

Caldwell, D H (ed). *Angels, Nobles and Unicorns*, Edinburgh, 1982.

Caldwell, D H and R Marshall. *The Queen's World: a Celebration of Mary Queen of Scots*, Edinburgh, 1987.

Carter, J and J Rae. *The Chambers Guide to Traditional Scottish Crafts*, Edinburgh, 1988.

Cheape, H, G Dalgleish, E Wright and J Kidd. *At Home: Ten Years Collecting from Historic Scotland*, Edinburgh, 1984.

Collinson, F. *The Traditional and National Music of Scotland*, London, 1966.

Dalgleish, G and D Mechan. *'I Am Come Home': Treasure of Prince Charles Edward Stuart*, Edinburgh, 1985.

Dalgleish, G and S Maxwell. *The Lovable Craft 1687–1987*, Edinburgh, 1987.

Dunbar, J. *The Historic Architecture of Scotland*, 2nd edition, London, 1978.

Evans, G. *French Connections: Scotland and the Arts of France*, Edinburgh, 1985.

Finlay, I. *Art in Scotland*, London, 1948.

Finlay, I. *Scottish Crafts*, London, 1948.

Hutchison, R E and S Maxwell. *A History of Scottish Costume*, Edinburgh, 1962.

Norman, A V B. *Arms and Armour in the Royal Scottish Museums*, Edinburgh, 1972.

Rowan, A. *The Creation of Shambellie: the Story of a Victorian Building Contract*, Edinburgh, 1982.

Stevenson, J H and M Wood. *Scottish Heraldic Seals*, Glasgow, 1946.

Stewart, C. *Holy Greed: the Forming of a Collection*, Edinburgh, 1981.

Stewart, I H. *The Scottish Coinage*, London, 1967.

Tarrant, N. *The Royal Scottish Museum Samplers*, Edinburgh, 1978.

Tarrant, N. *Costume in Scotland through the Ages*, Glasgow, 1986.

Geology and natural history

Andrews, S M. *The Discovery of Fossil Fishes in Scotland up to 1845 with a Checklist of Agassiz's Figured Specimens*, Edinburgh, 1982.

Chambers, S. *Polychaetes from Scottish Waters 2*, Edinburgh, 1982.

Baird, W J. *The Scenery of Scotland: The Structure Beneath*, Edinburgh, 1988.

Bunyan, I. *Polar Scots*, Spotlight Pack, Edinburgh, 1986.

Heddle, M F. *The Mineralogy of Scotland*, Edinburgh, 1989.

McCallion, W J. *Scottish Gem Stones*, Glasgow, 1937.

Macpherson, H G. *Agates*, Edinburgh and London, 1989.

Staces, H E, C W A Pettitt and C D Waterston (eds). *Natural Science Collections in Scotland*, Edinburgh, 1988.

Tebble, N and S Chambers. *Polychaetes of Scottish Waters 1*, Edinburgh, 1982.

In addition, the Royal Scottish Museum Information Series (1970 to 1985) and the National Museums of Scotland Information Series (from 1988) include lists and catalogues of geological and zoological material in the National Museums' collections.

Science, technology and industry

Anderson, R G W. *The Playfair Collection*, Edinburgh, 1978.

Bremner, D. *The Industries of Scotland*, Edinburgh, 1869, reprinted Newton Abbot, 1969.

Bryden, D J. *Scottish Scientific Instrument Makers 1600–1900*, Royal Scottish Museum Information Series Technology 1, Edinburgh, 1972.

Bunyan, I, J D Storer and C L Thompson. *East Fortune: Museum of Flight and History of the Airfield*, Edinburgh, 1983.

Campbell, R H. *The Rise and Fall of Scottish Industry*, Edinburgh, 1980.

Clement, A G and R H S Robertson. *Scotland's Scientific Heritage*, Edinburgh and London, 1961.

Hay, G D and G P Stell. *Monuments of Industry*, Edinburgh, 1986.

Hume, J R. *The Industrial Archaeology of Scotland*, vol I *The Lowlands and Borders*, London, 1976, vol II *The Highlands and Islands*, London, 1977.

Hume, J R and M S Moss. *Beardmore: The History of a Scottish Industrial Giant*, London, 1979.

Morrison-Low A D and J R R Christie (ed). *'Martyr of Science': Sir David Brewster 1781–1868*, Edinburgh, 1984.

Moss, M S and J R Hume. *Workshop of the British Empire*, London, 1977.

Simpson, A D C (ed). *Joseph Black 1728–1799*, Edinburgh, 1978.

Simpson, A D C and R G W Anderson. *Edinburgh and Medicine*, Edinburgh, 1976.

Slaven, A. *The Development of the West of Scotland*, London, 1975.

INDEX

Contributors

Dr R G W Anderson	Director
Dr S M Andrews	Curator, Vertebrate Fossils
W J Baird	Curator, Invertebrate Fossils and Fossil Plants
D J Bryden	Keeper, Department of Science, Technology and Working Life
Charles J Burnett	Curator, Scottish United Services Museum
Jenni Calder	Publications Officer
Dr David Caldwell	Curator, Scottish Medieval History
Allan Carswell	Curator, Scottish United Services Museum
Hugh Cheape	Curator, Scottish Modern History
Dr David V Clarke	Keeper, Department of Archaeology
George Dalgleish	Curator, Scottish Modern History
Dr Alexander Fenton	Research Director
Brian Jackson	Curator, Minerals and Gemstones
Dorothy Kidd	Scottish Ethnological Archive
Dr A Livingstone	Curator, X-ray Mineralogy
Dr H G Macpherson	Deputy Keeper, Department of Geology (retired)
R J Major	Curator, Museum of Flight
Dr W D I Rolfe	Keeper, Department of Geology
Dr G E Rotheray	Curator, Insects
Dr Alison Sheridan	Curator, Scottish Archaeology
R M Spearman	Curator, Scottish Archaeology
Gavin Sprott	Curator, Working Life and Scottish Agricultural Museum
Geoffrey N Swinney	Curator, Fish, Reptiles and Amphibians
Naomi Tarrant	Curator, Costume and Textiles
James L Wood	Curator, Engineering and Industry
Stephen Wood	Keeper, Scottish United Services Museum
Elizabeth Wright	Curator, Scottish Modern History

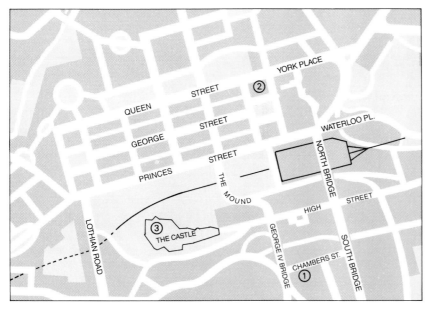

The National Museums of Scotland

1 Royal Museum of Scotland
Chambers Street

International collections of archaeology, decorative arts, ethnography, geology, natural history, science and technology, including some Scottish material.

2 Royal Museum of Scotland
Queen Street

Scottish archaeology, decorative arts, history; Scottish Ethnological Archive.

3 Scottish United Services Museum   Edinburgh Castle

Scottish military art, decorations, uniform and weapons.

4 Scottish Agricultural Museum
Ingliston

Scottish farming, fishing and rural life.

5 Museum of Flight
East Fortune

International collections of aircraft, aero engines and rockets, including Scottish material.

6 Shambellie House Museum of Costume   New Abbey

International and Scottish costume.

7 Biggar Gasworks Museum

Scottish small town gasworks and related material.